TURKISH NATIONALISM:

GREY WOLF MOVEMENT

Table of Contents

Dedication

At the beginning of my work, I feel it is my duty to gratefully remember our statesmen who labored for the unity of the Turkish nation, which has been separated for centuries, and for the construction of a "united and whole Turkish World." ALPARSLAN TÜRKEŞ, DEVLET BAHÇELİ, EBULFEZ ELÇİBEY, HAYDAR ALIYEV, ILHAM ALIYEV, NURSULTAN NAZARBAYEV, RECEP TAYYİP ERDOĞAN, SÜLEYMAN DEMİREL, ŞEVKET MIRZIYOYEV, TURGUT ÖZAL...

The flag you have raised will never fall. It will rise a little higher every day. "The Turkish World from the Adriatic to the Great Wall of China" was a dream yesterday. Today, it is as close as reality. Tomorrow, it will be the reality itself.

I dedicate this work to our great leader Alparslan Türkeş, who made us love the Turks, taught us about the captive Turks, and whose name I proudly bear, and to his worthy successor, Devlet Bahçeli. The effort is ours, the appreciation is from our nation, and the success is from Allah.

Preface

The Turks are the most ancient nation in history. The Turks, who have spread across vast territories, have established states all around the world. From the earliest known periods, Turks have shown a strong commitment to their tribe, nation, tradition, and homeland. Turks have been dynamic since ancient times, and they have had a high adaptability to changes. Recognizing that animal husbandry was more advantageous than hunting, the Proto-Turks domesticated deer, setting themselves apart from other communities. When they realized that it was easier to raise animals on the steppes and plains, they abandoned the forests they had lived in for centuries. Russians and Germans would abandon the forests thousands of years later. When they saw that breeding horses on the steppe was more advantageous, they domesticated horses. The domestication of the horse marked the beginning of centuries of Turkish dominance. Being involved in animal husbandry and spreading across vast territories, Turks discovered many minerals. As the world's first mining nation, they excelled in various minerals, especially copper, iron, and bronze, giving them a significant advantage in weaponry technology. As a result, the states established by Turks were among the world's most powerful states until the early 18th century. The Huns, Saka, Avars, and Göktürks were nomadic empires and were superpowers in their eras. When Turks arrived in South Central Asia, Khurasan, Iran, Azerbaijan, Anatolia, and the Middle East, they founded sedentary empires based on agriculture and trade, as they found that animal husbandry was not viable in these lands like the steppes. They developed a different land tenure system and land grant system from what had been practiced until then, maintaining their superiority. In the 10th century, the Ghaznavids, in the 11th century, the Seljuks, in the 12th century, the Turkic-Mongol Empire, in the 13th century, the Mamluks and the Golden Horde, in the 14th century, Timurids, and in the 15th, 16th, and 17th centuries, the Ottomans were superpowers. Except for the Ottomans, Turks began to decline from the early 16th century onwards. The Ottomans also began to decline from the 18th century. Turks, who had preserved their strong position in previous periods thanks to their ability to adapt to changes, could not achieve this anymore. They could not keep up with technological advancements and failed to adapt to the new economic order. Despite all efforts and struggles, they couldn't recover. In 1920, except for a narrow region in Eastern and Southeastern Anatolia, all Turkish territories were under occupation. In the last quarter of the 19th century, an awakening under the guidance of Turkish nationalism began. Ottoman Turkish nationalists aimed to save the empire from collapsing, Russian Turkish nationalists intended first to enlighten the Turks and then unite them after gaining their independence. Neither the empire could be saved nor could Russian Turks achieve independence. From this awakening and effort, the War of Independence emerged. Under the leadership of Atatürk, the Republic of Turkey was founded. The Idealist Movement, initiated by Türkeş, based on Turkishness and Islam, became the most influential movement of the last fifty years. The Idealist Movement aimed to develop Turkey. Without causing harm to Turkey, they tried to establish as close and intense relations as possible with external Turks. The nationalism adopted by the Idealists is inclusive, not divisive. It is unifying, not separatist. It is anti-imperialist. It is humane. It considers all nations as distinguished members of the human family. It does not claim superiority. Idealism is loving the Turkish nation and serving it. Before 1980, Turkey was under the threat of the Soviet Union. Communist supporters, who failed to come to power through a military coup, began street movements by arming themselves. The threat was serious. In the last quarter of a century, the Soviet Union had personally invaded many countries and supported regime changes in many countries. Idealists did not allow communists to make a revolution, take over the country, even if it meant risking their lives. Thanks to the struggles waged, the Soviet Union collapsed. New Turkish states were established. Turks took an important step toward unification by establishing the Organization of Turkish States. Hopefully, we will see that the 21st century is the Turkish century. The Turkish nation will once again carry the flag of Islam. It will be instrumental in bringing peace and justice to humanity. I wish not only Turks but every nation had idealists... I dedicate this work to our head teacher, Alparslan Türkeş, who made us love being Turkish and taught captive Turks. Effort is from us, appreciation is from our nation, and success is from Allah.

A-) THE FORMATION OF NATIONALISM THOUGHT

The sense of nationalism is inherent in humans. People have, since ancient times, loved and embraced their families, just as they love the society they are born into and adopt its values. They strive to elevate and protect the society they belong to, even sacrificing their lives for the people they live with when necessary. Among the nations that have preserved their existence today, the Turkish nation is the first to appear on the historical stage. The Turkish nation has managed to preserve and develop its existence because it has been able to maintain its unity and adapt to changes, even being pioneers of change for many centuries.

Nationalism as a systematic ideology emerged in recent times, but the feeling of nationalism has existed for centuries, from the moment nations were formed. It exists in nations like the Turks, who have existed for more than three thousand years, as well as in recently formed nations. In fact, the process of becoming a nation is still ongoing in some communities.

Today's Turks undoubtedly descend from the Huns, Saka, and Göktürks. However, due to migrations, wars, the acceptance of different religions, and marriages, their biological and cultural characteristics have undergone changes. On the other hand, the emergence of Turkish nationalism in a modern sense is related to developments in the West, but one can observe manifestations of Turkish nationalism in Turkish history. In other words, Turkish nationalism is modern, born in modern times, but it has taken shape within the framework of the national spirit that has evolved over thousands of years.

In modern times, the nationalist ideology that emerged can be divided into two main categories. One is the unity of individuals who make up a nation coming together towards common goals and forming a state through citizenship. The other is the dominance of individuals belonging to the same ethnicity, based on the common values of that ethnic group, over a piece of land (homeland, country, etc.). Therefore, in the context of social sciences, the two fundamental concepts are ethnicity and citizenship. Based on the time of their emergence, nationalist movements can be classified as follows.

Nationalisms Arising in Response to Colonization

As the renowned social scientist Benedict Anderson pointed out, movements aimed at establishing independent nation-states first emerged in the late 18th century in the Spanish colonies in Central and South America. In these colonies, there were groups of Spanish-origin elites known as the "Creoles" who lived there and administered the colonies on behalf of the Spanish crown. They challenged colonial central authority by mobilizing the indigenous populations. The Spanish implemented an unprecedented "social hierarchy scheme" in the Americas. At the top of this hierarchy were the nobles born in Spain. Below them were soldiers and civilian officials also born in Spain but not of noble origin. Those at the top of the hierarchy, including nobles and non-noble soldiers and officials, were born in Spain and were sent to America as a form of exile. Their goal was not the development, progress, or civilization of this region; instead, their aim was to collect as much tax revenue as possible and send it to the center to gain favor with the King and advance to high-ranking positions in Spain.

Spaniards who were merchants aimed to become wealthy quickly. If they stayed in America for a long time and had children there, their children would be Creoles and thus excluded. Even noble-born Creoles were considered lower in status than non-noble Spaniards. Creoles born in America were considered nobles but, when they returned to Spain, regardless of their wealth or their parents' status, they were regarded as inferior. Below the Creoles of noble origin, there were non-noble Creoles who were born in America. Their parents were Spanish, but they were not of noble origin. Below them were the mestizos, born to Spanish fathers and indigenous mothers. Below them were mestizos with African mothers. Subsequently, there were classifications for individuals such as indigenous people who were born as Christians, African slaves born as Christians, indigenous slaves who converted to Christianity, African slaves who converted to Christianity, non-Christian mestizo slaves, non-Christian African slaves, and non-Christian indigenous people. The indigenous people at the very bottom of this hierarchy could be killed for entertainment, and those who killed non-Christian indigenous people would not face punishment. If the killers were the owners, there was no issue, but if someone else killed them, the case would be closed if they compensated the owners for their loss. The fact that non-Christian slaves and indigenous people could be killed quickly led to the rapid Christianization of society. The possibility of being killed, even if they were not willing, led people to become Christians to secure their lives. The children or grandchildren of those who were Christian in appearance or at heart would become genuine Christians. Since both Spaniards and Creoles spoke only Spanish and had no knowledge of any other languages, other groups living with them learned Spanish and adopted Latin culture. While the society was rapidly assimilating in terms of language, religion, sect, and culture, due to the hierarchical system imposed, people became increasingly alienated from each other and from Spain. Since there were no firearms, ammunition, cannons, or rifles for slaves and indigenous people to confront Spaniards and Creoles, there were constant slave uprisings. However, slaves and indigenous people did not have the weapons necessary to confront Spaniards and Creoles, so while society was becoming more culturally similar, it was growing more hostile towards both each other and Spain.

Naturally, the wealthiest individuals in the continent were the Creoles. Moreover, since the resources of the Americas seemed inexhaustible, the Creoles were even wealthier than the Spaniards. Despite this, not even an ordinary Spaniard would give their daughter's hand in marriage to a Creole, even if the Creole's parents were noble.

Creoles could only marry or have relationships with others of their own kind, mestizos, indigenous people, or Africans. Children born from these relationships would also be marginalized. Due to the hierarchical system in place, the lower strata of society, including mestizos, were increasing in population. Both Creoles and lower-status mestizos, Africans, and indigenous people found no advantage in being connected to Spain. Because of this, Creoles, who were of Spanish origin, initiated a struggle to achieve their freedom by establishing independent administrative units. The fact that Creoles were of Spanish origin and that Spanish was the common language of Central and South America did not prevent the Spanish colonial order from continuing. After decades of struggle and warfare, nation-states were established one after another. Creoles, being bourgeoisie, became the driving force behind the independence movements in Latin America. In fact, Bolivar aimed to take the nationalist movement that aimed to gain independence from Spain a step further by establishing a common state called the "Union of Latin American States," but he could not garner enough support to achieve this goal. In other words, Latin American nationalism against colonial Spain did not acquire a unifying character.

In Portugal, although there was no system like in Spain, a regime based on racial discrimination was established in Brazil. Marriages were primarily arranged between white individuals. In other words, most mulattos born to white fathers were considered illegitimate. Even aristocratic families would not marry their daughters to Africans, mulattos, or indigenous people. Therefore, if noble girls could not find a suitable white husband, they were sent to convents in Europe. Banks would not give credit to mulattos, and they could not obtain licenses to open businesses. In other words, mulattos could work alongside white individuals and become managers or overseers on farms. In 1800, Brazil's population was approximately four million, with about 60% being free and 40% enslaved. When Napoleon invaded Portugal, the King fled to Brazil, making Rio de Janeiro the center of the empire. In 1815, Brazil was given the same status as Portugal. In 1819, following Napoleon's definitive defeat, the Emperor appointed his son Don Pedro as the general governor and ruled Latin America from Brazil until his return to Portugal. In 1822, when the Portuguese parliament decided to nullify Brazil's equal status and return it to colonial status, Don Pedro initiated a rebellion. The rebellion resulted in the establishment of the independent Brazilian

Empire in 1824. The leader of the rebellion was the son of the Portuguese King.

Another movement of the same type that developed concurrently with nationalism in Latin America but achieved success earlier was American nationalism. The reason behind the separatist movement against the United Kingdom, led by the leading political and economic elites of the British colonies in North America, was the central authority's constant imposition of new financial burdens on the colonial populations by exploiting the region's natural and human resources. From the mid-1700s, there were four fundamental areas of disagreement and conflicting interests between the Kingdom and the colonies. If the king of the time had been more foresighted, the problems could have been resolved without war, division, and through a peaceful transition. (Britain learned from the American process and applied softer policies in Canada, Australia, and New Zealand.) The most important problem was the issue of representation. The colonies were populous, and constant immigration led to rapid population growth. However, the colonies had no representation in the British Parliament. The decisions of the Parliament bound the colonies, yet the colonies had no say in these decisions. In fact, there were local assemblies in the colonies, and these local assemblies could have been empowered to become national assemblies accountable to the monarch. The second issue was the new taxes imposed by England on the colonies and the regulations it implemented in the late period. England's participation in consecutive wars at that time strained its budget. Members of parliament who believed that increasing taxes in England would lead to their defeat in elections found a solution in raising taxes in the colonies and passing regulations that would make the colonies cover some expenses that were previously covered by the treasury. These measures were met with strong opposition. In fact, if the first problem had been resolved, the second one would not have occurred. The other significant problem was wars. When England went to war in Europe, the colonies were involuntarily drawn into wars that had nothing to do with them. When England fought against France or Spain, the colonies found themselves fighting against French and Spanish forces in America without reason. Their economies suffered, and their sons died. When the wars ended, the colonies, whose opinions were not considered during the treaty negotiations, had to abide by the terms of the treaties. The fourth important issue was the desire of the colonial populations to expand westward and become wealthier. Vast lands lay to the west, and the colonies wanted to expand. Since the king did not want to deal with Native Americans or the French in the west, he did not allow expansion. These problems, along with others of lesser importance, became chronic as they went unresolved for a long time. Independence movements in the colonies gained strength. Eventually, rebellion and civil war broke out, leading to independence.

When the colonies became independent, they did not immediately move towards political integration to establish a common state. It is worth noting that the Declaration of Independence was signed in 1783, but the first president, George Washington, was elected in 1789. Initially, the thirteen colonies acted like independent states. Each issued its own currency, formed its own army, and imposed taxes. Local parliaments passed laws. However, they soon faced economic collapse and found themselves in a situation where they could go to war with each other. The colonies' economies were integrated into the British colonial empire. When England started the independence war, it stopped buying raw materials from the colonies. Naturally, the economies that were based on the sale of raw materials collapsed. Since consumer goods were imported from England, shortages began to occur. Since each colony collected taxes on goods coming from other colonies, establishing production facilities did not make economic sense. The states were not so densely populated. The major problem after the economic collapse was the westward expansion policy. When the king's restriction was lifted, the colonies turned westward. When multiple colonies simultaneously claimed the same territories, conflicts arose. To revive their economies and manage westward expansion, they needed a central authority. The colonies had a significant advantage at this point. The colonies had formed a continental assembly to conduct the independence war collectively. After the victory, the assembly disbanded. The Virginia colony called for a meeting and announced that it would send George Washington as a delegate to the meeting to represent Virginia. Washington was respected because he was the victorious commander-in-chief. The gathered delegates debated and exchanged ideas for two years. They eventually published a declaration of rights and then declared the establishment of the United States, electing Washington as the first president. The majority of the population in American colonies were of British descent. Therefore, in the United States, the dominant ethnic and cultural group became the White Anglo-Saxon

Protestants. Furthermore, the United States is a prime example of how a shared destiny and future ideal, dominated by a common ethnic identity, came to prevail in terms of national unity.

Nationalist movements in America constituted the first wave of what is called anti-imperialist nationalism or anti-colonial nationalism. The common feature of this wave is that groups belonging to the ethnic core of the dominant imperial structure but living in different geographic locations fight for independence against the central authority, which we can refer to as the homeland. Europeans protested against European imperialism.

The second wave of anti-colonial nationalisms, covering the first seventy years of the 20th century, took place in Asia and Africa. This time, indigenous peoples living under colonial and mandate administrations in Asia and Africa rebelled against colonial administrations and demanded their national independence. In this regard, nationalist movements that could be described as fully anti-imperialist began to emerge in the second half of the 20th century, leading to a change in the political map of the "Old World" and the establishment of many new nation-states.

In most of these countries, the presence of economic elites representing the former colonial powers and the active economic and trade relationships maintained with these elites continue to demonstrate that ultimate independence has not yet been achieved in terms of complete economic sovereignty. Additionally, with some exceptions, the borders of these newly independent states were defined by the colonial powers. These borders did not necessarily reflect the divisions among the local populations. Colonialists occupied lands they deemed profitable and established colonial rule over those lands. When the people living on those lands fought against the colonialists and achieved independence, they had to accept the borders that were determined by the colonialists. As a result, people speaking different languages became citizens of the same state, and people speaking the same language found themselves living in different states. This situation has led to numerous internal conflicts, civil wars, coups, revolutions, and genocidal massacres in Africa. Sudan and Ethiopia were divided, resulting from differences in the religion of the separating populations. South Sudan and Eritrea emerged as independent states. In South Africa, the white ethnic group (mostly of British and Dutch origin), which gained independence from the United

Kingdom through a nationalist movement, implemented apartheid (racial segregation) policies that oppressed the black majority for many years. The successful struggle for equal rights led by Nelson Mandela and the black majority changed the course of history and created an example of two different anti-colonial nationalisms succeeding one another.

As Africans began to make more intensive and systematic efforts to gain economic independence in the 2000s, they found Turkey alongside them.

Unifying Nationalisms

Uniting nationalism, as a concept, refers to the efforts of an ethnic group that has not yet achieved national unity to unite the members of various local groups scattered across a specific geographical area under a single administrative unit and common citizenship to establish a nation-state centered around that ethnic or cultural identity. In this case, different local groups belonging to the same ethnic or cultural identity organize themselves around this identity and, after gaining independence from the imperial structure or structures they were subject to, all local groups unite on a common homeland to establish a new nation-state. The best-known examples of such unifying nationalist movements are the 19th-century Italian and German national unification movements.

After the fall of the Roman Empire, Italy existed as a collection of city-states for centuries. The common factor among the people was the Italian language. Large parts of Italian territory were under the control of the Austro-Hungarian Empire. Count Cavour, the leader of the Kingdom of Piedmont, which became the most powerful Italian state after the fall of Venice by Napoleon, led the way to the establishment of an independent and united Italy. It was impossible for Piedmont to deal with Austria-Hungary on its own. Therefore, they first gained the support of European public opinion. By participating alongside England and France with the Ottoman Empire in the Crimean War against the Russian Empire, they attracted the attention of the peoples and statesmen of Europe. First, some city-states voluntarily joined Piedmont. With the nationalist army of volunteers led by Garibaldi, Naples and Sicily were captured. First, alliances were established with Germany and then with France to participate in the wars fought by these states against Austria-Hungary. In these wars, regions such as Venice and Lombardy joined Italy. (After the defeat of Napoleon, independent Venice was not allowed to be reestablished, and Venice's territories were given to Austria-Hungary.) Finally, in 1871, the Papal State centered in Rome was also abolished, and Italian unity was established.

The Germans had been living in city-states for centuries. The great powers of Europe opposed the unification of the Germans and the establishment of a united and therefore powerful Germany. The rulers and nobles of the German states were against a united Germany because they would lose their positions. The German people, especially after the occupation by Napoleon, became aware of their "German identity." The humiliation they suffered due to the occupation made the Germans want a powerful state to avoid similar situations in the future. Napoleon's destruction of the feudal land regime based on aristocracy facilitated the establishment of German unity. Although attempts were made to re-establish the old system after Napoleon, they were never successful. The number of German city-states increased or decreased according to the agreements made by the great powers of Europe after wars. Many German city-states were under the influence of Austria-Hungary and France. Austria-Hungary was a multi-ethnic empire ruled by a German dynasty. About 20% of its population was German. No one ever said "Germany." When you asked where Vienna was going, everyone said Austria. No one said Germany. When you asked where Berlin was going, everyone said Prussia. No one said Germany. So where was Germany? Germany was nowhere. The academician-turned-politician Friedrich List argued that in order for German unity to be established, economic unity must first be achieved. No German statelet would accept the authority of another. They would not give up their existence voluntarily. The conquest of the powerful German states by the weaker ones could only sow the seeds of hostility among the Germans. It would strengthen sub-identities like Bavarianism, Bohemianism, and Prussianism. The establishment of a customs union among the German states was the indispensable prerequisite for the German Customs Union project. This would not only solve the problem of division but also the problem of backwardness. Although Germans were more populous than the French and the British, they could not form a single market because they were divided among themselves. The Customs Union also meant a market of 50 million. This would make German producers competitive. The indispensable part of the German Customs Union project was that the German states be connected to each other by railways. Thus, transportation costs would decrease, and the Germans would be able to reach each other quickly and easily. Some of the German states formed a Customs Union among themselves with the efforts of Friedrich List. When these states achieved high rates of development, others joined them voluntarily. In both unifying nationalist movements, there was a leading state (Piedmont and Prussia) that aimed to establish an administrative unit by uniting the administrative units.

We mentioned earlier the American colonies' fight for independence from England as an example of anti-colonial nationalism. After the American War of Independence, each of the 13 British colonies gained independence. However, they both had conflicts and problems among themselves and could not prosper individually. After this period, the colonial leaders convened a congress and established the United States, electing Washington as their president. The establishment of the United States of America during this period is one of the most successful examples of unifying nationalism.

Racist Nationalisms

Racist nationalism manifests in two different forms: one within a state where various ethnic-racial groups coexist under the umbrella of a single nation, and the other between different administrative states where dominant ethnic cores are composed of distinct ethnic-racial groups. In the first scenario, an ethnic identity is elevated through racial discourse, leading to discrimination against other racial groups within the administrative structure. In response, these marginalized groups organize and struggle on ethnic-racial grounds. Prime examples of this form of racist nationalism can be found in the recent history of the United States' southern states and South Africa, where discrimination against black populations was prevalent. Although legally, citizens now have equal rights, racist groups and ideologies have continued to have some significance and social support, particularly in the southern regions of the United States. Organizations like the Ku Klux Klan and similar racist groups espouse the belief that white Aryans are the rightful owners of the country, contrasting with ethnic groups such as blacks, Jews, and Chinese. This illustrates the ideological content of such racist nationalisms. While these organizations have lost some of their past social support, they still find followers, especially in the southern states of the United States.

The second type of situation where racist nationalism takes root involves international relations. One of the best examples of this is Nazi nationalism that prevailed in Germany before and during World War II. In Nazi ideology, only the Aryan race was considered superior, and races not included in this category and their respective nations were labeled as inferior races by leading Nazi ideologues and Hitler. Nazi actions such as invasions of neighboring European countries inhabited by Slavic peoples and the implementation of Race Laws targeting Jewish, Slavic, and Romani citizens within Germany were based on this racist nationalist perspective. Nazis conducted propaganda campaigns emphasizing that the peoples of the occupied countries in Western Europe belonged to the same racial group, the Aryan race, as the Germans. They aimed to prevent resistance and uprisings in the occupied territories. Despite the common racial discourse, this approach failed to gain traction in countries where the majority of the population, including those from England, France, and the United States, did not identify with the Aryan race and actively opposed Nazi aggression.

Expansionist Nationalisms

Expansionist nationalism is similar to unifying nationalism in many ways, but it differs in one key aspect. Unifying nationalism aims to unite groups with common ethnic and cultural characteristics, often spread across a specific geographic area, in order to establish a nation-state. Expansionist nationalism, on the other hand, focuses on incorporating into an existing nation-state the groups living outside its borders, typically in neighboring regions, who share similar ethnic and cultural traits. Such forms of nationalism are generally referred to as Pan-nationalism. One of the best examples of this type of nationalism can be found in the era of Nazi Germany.

During the Nazi era, the presence of ethnic Germans living within the borders of neighboring countries such as Poland, Czechoslovakia, and France contradicted the Nazis' goal of German unity when they came to power in 1933. To address this, they aimed to create a living space, or Greater Germany, by invading neighboring countries and incorporating the ethnically German populations left outside the borders. Other examples of expansionist nationalism include the ideals of Greater Serbia, the Megali Idea of the Greeks, and Greater Albania.

In summary, expansionist nationalism seeks to expand the boundaries of a nation-state by incorporating ethnically and culturally similar groups living outside its existing borders, often under the banner of a pan-nationalist ideology.

Anti-Foreign Nationalisms

Xenophobic nationalism arises from the resentment harbored by a country's citizens toward people who have immigrated from foreign countries and settled there. In these forms of nationalism, factors such as the immigrants' differences in culture, language, ethnicity, race, and religion from the citizens make it easier for xenophobic nationalism to develop. Xenophobia has particularly gained prominence in Western European countries like France, England, Germany, the Netherlands, Austria, and Italy over the past quarter-century.

One of the most successful examples of this type of nationalism is the National Front movement in France, which has gained strength and followers in recent years, primarily by advocating a radical nationalist program against foreign-origin residents in the country, particularly settled Arabs from former French colonies. In the last two decades, xenophobia against people of Chinese descent has been on the rise, especially in East Asian countries like Korea and Japan, which have experienced an influx of immigrants from China. An interesting case of such hostility is directed towards recent Chinese immigrants in Singapore, where a majority of the population is of Chinese origin.

Xenophobic nationalism sometimes incorporates elements of racism, but in many European countries, laws against racism have led these movements to develop different narratives. These narratives often revolve around claims that immigrants, due to their role as cheap labor, hinder the employment opportunities of locals and have higher crime rates. These movements have managed to garner support from citizens, especially those from the lower and middle classes. Xenophobia tends to gain ground more easily in countries experiencing economic difficulties.

When considering demographic trends and migration patterns, it can be confidently stated that xenophobic nationalism is likely to continue strengthening in Europe in the coming years. Additionally, xenophobia against Chinese immigrants in Africa and Latin America is also expected to intensify.

Diaspora Nationalisms

Diaspora nationalism is a type of nationalism observed in ethnic-cultural groups living outside their homeland or the boundaries of a nation-state. This form of nationalism, conceptualized by the social scientist Ernest Gellner, encompasses not only ethnic but also socio-economic aspects. As Gellner illustrated using the example of the Jewish diaspora, some ethnic-cultural groups, through migration, establish specific socio-economic positions or occupy particular economic sectors in the countries where they have settled. In other words, they become a significant part of the local bourgeoisie and play a role in the social relations characterized by what Gellner referred to as "double standards." This double standard consists of attitudes and behaviors directed towards individuals from their own ethnic group and those outside the group, i.e., members of the larger society.

While maintaining loyalty to the country they live in, they also remain loyal to their homeland. They uphold a sense of solidarity with their fellow compatriots. This situation, which can be referred to as dual loyalty, allows for the preservation of two different types of nationalism: constitutional and ethnic. Gellner provides examples of various groups, such as Jews, Armenians, Greeks living in different countries; Chinese residing in various Southeast Asian nations, and Parsis of Iranian origin living in India, as instances of diaspora nationalism. In recent years, diaspora nationalisms among Turks in Western Europe and among Indians in the United States have been on the rise.

New Ethnic Nationalisms

Since the last quarter of the 20th century, a type of nationalism has been on the rise, especially after the collapse of the Eastern Bloc. This form of nationalism can be described as the resurgence of ethnic nationalism, often associated with separatist movements. The existence of these movements has led to a questioning of the inclusivity of the nation-state, demonstrating that ethnicity still holds sociological significance. When the ethnic group driving such a movement is not large in number, these movements are sometimes referred to as micro-nationalisms.

Examples of micro-nationalisms include the Chechens in the Caucasus fighting for independence from Russia, and the Abazins, Ossetians, and Adjarians in Georgia. Additionally, the Hutu-Tutsi conflict in Africa, which escalated to the level of mutual genocides and resulted in changes to the political map of Central Africa, represents a distinct example of new ethnic nationalisms. In this case, the Hutu and Tutsi ethnicities were not based on racial or cultural elements but stemmed from the colonial authorities in Central Africa classifying the region's population into Hutu and Tutsi based on physical characteristics such as height, beauty, and skin color during the French colonial period.

Another example of new ethnic nationalism can be found in Belgium, where the idea of establishing an independent state separate from the French-speaking Walloons, mainly located in the southern regions, has gained traction among the Dutch-speaking Flemish population residing in the northern regions. This phenomenon shows that ethnic nationalism can exist even within supranational entities like the European Union.

Other instances of micro-nationalism include the Corsicans in France seeking independence, the Lombards in Italy aiming for separation, and the Scots in the United Kingdom striving for independence. Undoubtedly, Catalan nationalism stands out as the most influential ethnic nationalism in Europe.

In Russia, ethnic nationalism is developing among the approximately thirty million Turkish communities, the majority of whom reside in autonomous republics. The development of nationalism among Russian Turks is, from a historical perspective, anti-colonial nationalism. However, when the Soviet Union collapsed, the Turks were a minority in their own homeland. Thus, ethnic nationalism was prevalent among Turks at that time. Over a period of thirty-two years, Turks in most autonomous republics became the majority. (According to estimates, by 2030, Turks will be the majority in all Turkish autonomous republics.) Therefore, for Turks living in these republics, anti-colonial nationalism applies. However, for the same individuals living in Russia, a different form of diaspora nationalism is also in play.

Assessment of Nationalist Movements in Historical and Geographical Perspectives

When we examine the historical and geographical distribution of nationalist movements, we encounter an interesting pattern that can be briefly summarized as follows:

In the 18th century, the first wave of nationalism was characterized by anti-colonial nationalisms in North and South America. Towards the late 18th century and the early 19th century, Western Europe saw the dominance of unifying nationalisms with a liberal orientation that aligned with the modern nation-state concept.

From the second quarter of the 19th century through the interwar period of World War I, ethnic nationalisms prevailed, particularly within multinational entities such as the Austro-Hungarian and Ottoman Empires. Various ethnic groups within these structures sought to break away and establish their own nation-states, resulting in the emergence of new nation-states in Europe and the Middle East.

During the interwar period between the two World Wars, fascist nationalisms led by countries like Germany, Spain, Portugal, and Italy initially rose and later declined.

The quarter-century following World War II was characterized by the end of colonial rule in Asia and Africa due to anti-colonial and anti-imperialist nationalist struggles by indigenous populations. This period saw the formation of new independent nation-states in these regions.

From the last quarter of the 20th century onwards, influenced by the collapse of the Eastern Bloc and the rise of globalization, ethnic and cultural identities regained importance both socially and politically. Especially in Eurasia, small-scale ethnic groups within nation-states led to the emergence of new ethnic, or micro-nationalisms, often associated with separatist demands.

This development led to academic debates about whether the nation-state remains the most modern and enduring administrative system in terms of inclusivity, representation, and unity, even as questions were raised about the nation-state's ability to encompass its citizens and adapt to changing global dynamics.

Furthermore, even within supranational entities like the European Union, the rise of separatist movements, as seen in the example of Belgium, deepened the questioning of the nation-state.

Nationalism has indeed played a significant role in the last two centuries of human history. While it is widely accepted that nation-states and nationalism are losing some of their significance in the face of globalization, the reality is more complex. Globalization has brought societies closer together, increased awareness of cultural differences, and emphasized the enduring importance of ethnic and national identities.

In addition to ethnic nationalisms, the persistence of expansionist nationalism, xenophobic nationalism, and racist nationalism in many countries demonstrates that nationalism remains relevant. These various forms of nationalism continue to find supporters, highlighting the enduring significance of nationalism in our globalized world.

B-) THE EMERGENCE OF TURKISH NATIONALISM IDEAS

In the final years of the Ottoman Empire, various ideas were being debated in an attempt to halt its decline. These ideas included Islamic nationalism, Ottomanism, and Turkism, all of which, despite appearing as rivals, had a nationalist spirit with the goal of saving the Turkish Empire from disintegration.

The separatist movements that began with the Greek uprising continued with the secession of Serbia, Romania, and Bulgaria from the Ottoman Empire. These developments weakened the Ottomanism idea and strengthened Islamic nationalism. However, Ottomanism did not completely disappear as a concept because a significant portion of the empire's population was non-Muslim.

During the reign of Sultan Mahmud II and later, the Ottoman Empire started to implement unnamed and unspoken nationalist policies. These policies became more widespread after the Tanzimat reforms and reached their peak during the reign of Sultan Abdulhamid II. The fundamental aim of these reforms initiated by Mahmud II was to improve the conditions of the Muslim population, particularly the Turks, who were considered to be lagging behind minorities. Initiatives included promoting education, increasing the number of Turkish-language publications, and making Turkish the language of education. These were among the key nationalist policies pursued during this period.

The non-Muslim minorities did not face the same problems with education. Missionary groups, primarily Catholic, Protestant, and Anglican denominations, had established hundreds of schools throughout the empire. In response, Ottoman Christians (Orthodox, Copts, Syriacs, Gregorians, and other groups) and Jews also opened their schools. Russia and Greece, especially, provided support to Orthodox Christians. Thousands of minority members received education in Russia and Greece. The first printing press in the Ottoman Empire was established by Jews during the late 15th century. In the 16th century, cities like Istanbul, Izmir, Edirne, and Thessaloniki had printing presses catering to Jews and, to some extent, Christians. The first Christian printing press for the Orthodox community was established in Edirne in 1567. After the first press, numerous printing presses were set up across the empire, and thousands of publications were produced. Missionary groups often initiated their activities by establishing printing presses.

Ibrahim Muteferrika established the first Turkish printing press in 1726, during the reign of Sultan Ahmed III. After printing about ten books, this press closed due to lack of interest. However, during the reign of Sultan Mahmud II and his successors, major efforts were made to establish Turkish-language schools, increase the production of Turkish-language books, newspapers, and magazines, and promote Turkish. As modern schools began teaching in Turkish, the weakening of Arabic (the language of education in madrasas) and the strengthening of Turkish became concurrent processes. These activities, which began during Sultan Mahmud II's reign, became even more systematic and widespread during the reign of Sultan Abdulhamid II. During his time, the goal was to educate Turkish citizens first, then Muslim citizens, followed by non-Turkic Muslims, and finally non-Muslim citizens. Simultaneously, efforts were made to create large groups of loyal citizens among the Christian and Jewish minorities.

Sultan Abdulhamid II, during his rule, seized the opportunity of the long period of peace that followed the Russo-Turkish War of 1877-1878, except for the successful outcome of the Greco-Turkish War. This period allowed the Ottoman Empire to recover. The migrations caused by the loss of territories, especially after the Treaty of Küçük Kaynarca in 1774, and later after the 1877-1878 war (known as the 93 War), increased nationalist consciousness. The loss of territories and these migrations contributed to strengthening the sense of Turkishness.

In 1908, with the declaration of the Second Constitutional Era, disturbing movements began to emerge. Ethnic separatists, including Armenian militias, initiated rebellions. To counter these developments, Ottomanism and Islamic nationalism were initially promoted and implemented. However, it became apparent that these ideologies alone could not prevent the disintegration of the empire. Intellectuals started looking for solutions, leading to the emergence of various ideas during this period. One of these ideas was Turkism.

Intellectuals who embraced Turkism founded the Turkish Hearth in 1912 and began systematic work under its umbrella. The most significant outcome of these efforts was the Turkish Homeland (Türk Yurdu) magazine, which became the voice of nationalism. Although it's not possible to claim that all members of the Turkish Hearth shared the same nationalist ideology, it's clear that two dominant ideas emerged: racial nationalism advocated by Yusuf Akçura and cultural nationalism developed by Ziya Gökalp.

Yusuf Akçura, originally from Tataristan, received education in military schools in Turkey. He was later exiled during Sultan Abdulhamid II's rule and received political science education in France. Upon his return to Tataristan, he played a role in the establishment of the Russian Muslim Alliance political party and tried to raise awareness among Turks through the Kazan Muhbiri newspaper. After the declaration of the Second Constitutional Era, he came to Istanbul and became one of the founders of the Turkish Hearth. He wrote articles for the Turkish Hearth magazine. In his article titled "Three Types of Policy," published in Egypt, Akçura discussed Ottomanism, Islamic nationalism, and Turkism. He argued that Turkism should be turned into a political program, becoming part of state policy. He wrote, "Turkish unity will unite Turks in the empire, representing in terms of religion and race, and it will also represent to some extent those who are not of Turkish origin but have become Turkified. The most important thing is to unite the dispersed Turks around the world and create a great political nation, which will be achieved through Turkism. The most powerful, advanced, and civilized among the Turkish communities, the Ottoman Empire, will play the essential role in this process."

In explaining Turkism, Akçura pointed out that Ottoman Turks were only concerned with the language and history of other Turks. He argued that this was not enough and that contemporary ideologies needed to be learned to accelerate the process of unification.

Please note that the translation provided is a summary of the text's content, and some details may be omitted for brevity.

Ziya Gökalp, representing the second main strand of thought, made significant contributions to the systematization of Turkish nationalism through his writings and articles in the "Türk Yurdu" (Turkish Homeland) magazine. According to Gökalp, "Turkism means elevating the Turkish nation. A nation is not defined by race, tribe, geography, politics, or administration. A nation is a cultural group composed of individuals who share a common language, religion, ethics, and aesthetics." Gökalp was also a member of the Committee of Union and Progress (CUP) and the Turkish Hearth (Türk Ocağı) organization. He shared his ideas with the Turkish nation through articles published in "Genç Kalemler," "Türk Yurdu," and "Yeni Mecmua" magazines. Gökalp emphasized the importance of Turkification in language and culture and advocated the idea of Turkification, Islamization, and modernization, which was proposed by Hüseyin Zade Ali Bey six years earlier.

Gökalp declared, "I am from the Turkish nation, I am from the Islamic community, and I am from Western civilization," to express his identity. He defined Turkism in three phases: Turkiyecilik (Turkishness), Oğuzculuk or Türkmencilik (Oghuz/Turkic identity), and Turancılık (Pan-Turkism). Gökalp argued that the concept of the Ottoman nation, encompassing everyone living within the Ottoman borders, was incorrect, and that such a definition of the nation could not be sustained. He defined a nation as those who share a common language, religion, ethics, and sense of beauty. He criticized the concept of a nation based on geography, emphasizing that a sociological definition based on race and ethnicity was not possible.

Gökalp stressed the importance of national consciousness and believed that the lack of it was the reason for the Islamic world's subjugation to colonial powers. He considered culture as the foundation of nationalism and highlighted that language was at the core of this cultural identity. Gökalp acknowledged religion as one of the components of a nation but pointed out that the concepts of nation and ummah (Islamic community) had different meanings.

Gökalp was one of the leading proponents of the Turan concept, defining Turan as the geographical region where Turks lived and Turkish was spoken. He viewed Turkism as a means to elevate the Turkish nation and emphasized the equality of all nations. He believed that Turkish nationalism was the prescription for salvation and attached importance to the harmony between religion and the nation. Gökalp argued that national sentiment led to cooperation, self-sacrifice, and the spirit of struggle. He saw any reluctance among Turks to embrace the nationalist ideal as harmful to the state and dangerous to the existence of Turkishness.

Apart from the two major thinkers whose views have been briefly expressed, other figures such as Gaspıralı Ismail Bey, Hüseyinzâde Ali Bey, Ağaoğlu Ahmet Bey, Sadri Maksudi Arsal, and Zeki Velidi Togan also played a significant role in spreading Turkish nationalism and interest in external Turkic peoples. Gaspıralı Ismail Bey, who emphasized "unity in language, thought, and action should always enlighten our path," initiated the Jadid movement and made significant contributions with his articles in the Tercüman newspaper and the establishment of modern schools across various corners of the Turkic world. His priority was to raise awareness among Muslims in Russia and educate enlightened generations. Gaspıralı believed in the need to learn valuable ideas from the West and modernize education while making Ottoman Turkish more accessible to the Turkic world. He emphasized the importance of education and the necessity of unifying the Turkish language under a single alphabet.

Gaspıralı also criticized the use of the term "Tatar" by Russia to divide the Turks, advocating for the use of the term "Turk" instead. He highlighted the importance of national consciousness as a prerequisite for the start of the national struggle and underscored its significance in nationalist theory. In Gaspıralı's definition of the nation, language and religion were essential components. He believed that a national sense of identity was crucial for the success of the nationalist movement.

Hüseyinzâde Ali Bey, an Azerbaijani-born thinker, played a pioneering role in cultural and political Turkish nationalism. He was a member of the Committee of Union and Progress and one of the founders of the Turkish Hearth. He made significant contributions to nationalist theory. Although he had a medical education, Hüseyinzâde Ali Bey used newspapers like "Hayat" and "Fuyuzat" in Azerbaijan and Tiflis to spread his ideas and advocate against the policies of Iranianization and Russification. He introduced the synthesis of Turkification, Islamization, and Europeanization, presenting a new approach. Ali Bey argued that Ottoman Turkish should be the common language of the Turks, and he defined the nation as those who spoke Turkish, were Muslim, and identified themselves as Turkish.

In summary, these thinkers, including Ziya Gökalp, contributed to the development and spread of Turkish nationalism, emphasizing various aspects of national identity, language, and culture. They played crucial roles in shaping the intellectual foundations of Turkish nationalism and its influence on different segments of society.

Ağaoğlu Ahmet Bey, who represented Azerbaijan in the committee established following the 1905 revolution in Russia and tasked with resolving the "Nationalities Question," wrote influential articles defending and explaining Turkish nationalism from the first issue of the "Türk Yurdu" (Turkish Homeland) magazine. Born in Shusha, Ağaoğlu received his education in Russia and later studied law, history, and political science in France. After returning to Azerbaijan in 1894, he shared his ideas with the Azerbaijani Turks through newspapers such as İrşad, Terakki, and Fuyuzat. When Ahmet Ağaoğlu visited Turkey during the Second Constitutional Period, he particularly emphasized Turkism and modernity in his articles. He highlighted the necessity of national consciousness for the survival of the Turkish people and argued that Turkism and Islam were not contradictory. In his work titled "Üç Medeniyet" (Three Civilizations), he emphasized the importance of language skills and pointed out that Western intellectuals knew English, German, French, and even Greek and Latin, whereas Turks were lacking in this regard. Ağaoğlu's articles also emphasized the concept of morality, which he defined as loyalty, fidelity, selflessness, love of justice, and a passion for truth. He argued that individuals needed to overcome egoism and that defining the state through the nation was correct, as it could not be based on clans or families. Ağaoğlu defined a nation as a community sharing the same language, customs, beliefs, common history, homeland, and common destiny. He highlighted the harmony between religion and nationality, considering them as complementary concepts and identified tribalism and clan-based loyalties as the main enemies of the nation and nationalism.

Sadri Maksudi Arsal, born in Tatarstan, received his education in Russia and France. Arsal came to Turkey shortly after the proclamation of the Republic and shared his ideas with the Turkish nation through conferences, articles, and books. Arsal emphasized the simplification of the Turkish language and the development of a common language and alphabet among Turkic communities. He believed that the source of the national idea was the sense of loyalty that individuals felt towards the group to which they belonged. Arsal argued that, in order to survive, people needed to struggle and cooperate in groups. He emphasized the human need to live in peace within the framework of psychological development and stated that the national consciousness was crucial for nations to live as nations, preventing them from dissolving or disappearing into other nations. He defined national consciousness as the sense of deep attachment individuals felt toward their nation's history, future, language, culture, homeland, and shared destiny. He influenced many Turkish nationalists, especially those educated in Russia, as the awakening of national consciousness was a common experience among minority communities living under oppression. These intellectuals sought refuge in the Ottoman Empire, where they shared their ideas with Ottoman intellectuals and youth, contributing to the spread of the idea of Pan-Turkism.

Turkish nationalists were unable to prevent the collapse of the Ottoman Empire but played a significant role in the establishment of the Republic of Turkey. During the transition from the Empire to the nation-state, the idea of nationalism, particularly the understanding represented by Ziya Gökalp, influenced the ideas of both Mustafa Kemal Atatürk and Alparslan Türkeş. Türkeş, who referred to Ziya Gökalp as the "intellectual father" of Atatürk, stated, "The path of Turkish nationalism is one that derives strength from Ziya Gökalp Bey. Of course, the days we live in have brought new conditions. Principles will be adjusted according to these new conditions. However, the main foundation remains unchanged: Turkification, Islamization, and modernization are still fundamental ideas today." Türkeş was influenced by several intellectual figures, including Atsız, Mümtaz Turhan, Nurettin Topçu, Erol Güngör, Nejdet Sancar, Osman Turan, Osman Yüksel Serdengeçti, İbrahim Kafesoğlu, and Seyyit Ahmet Arvasi. Even during his childhood, as a young person who had experienced the Greek oppression during the British occupation, Türkeş empathized with the suffering of millions of Turks under foreign rule. While studying at

Kuleli Military High School, he became acquainted with Atsız's ideas. Atsız's poems, novels, and articles were influential in shaping Türkeş's understanding of Turkism. Later, Türkeş had personal meetings with Atsız, and these encounters, along with the discussions they had, contributed to the development of his intellectual foundation and determination for struggle.

Pan-Turkism (Turancılık)

We refer to the utopia that establishes a sense of Turkic identity, based on a common history, culture, language, and even territorial integrity, as "Turan." The concept of Turanism, attributed to Hüseyinzade Ali Bey, a medical student in 1892, was of significant importance during the transition from the Ottoman Empire to the national homeland. Particularly after the trauma experienced by Turks following the Balkan Wars, the concept of Turanism held a compensatory place for the Turks, who were the essential component of the multi-ethnic, multilingual, and multi-religious cosmopolitan structure of the Ottoman Empire, based on the loyalty of minority populations. One of the reasons for the prevalence of Turanism among the Turks was their existential concerns. Turkish nationalists under the influence of Russian-born intellectuals were worried about the "Russophobia" (fear of Russia) and the desire to liberate their occupied homelands. These Russian-origin Turkish nationalists were concerned not only because they feared that the Ottoman Empire would share the same fate as their own homelands but also because they saw that steps were being taken in that direction. The partition plans for the Ottoman Empire were on the rise during that period. Ömer Seyfettin, the author of the famous quote "The natural boundaries of a state are not mountains and rivers, but the linguistic and religious boundaries of the nationality it claims," rejected nationalism based on ethnicity and proposed the unification of Turkish territories in Central Asia under the Ottoman banner. He also worked on the idea of Turanism in his works, contributing to the widespread acceptance of this concept.

The figure who translated the idea of Turkish nationalism into the political arena was Yusuf Akçura. Turkish nationalism emerged as a reactionary response against Russia, but it transformed into the concept of "İttihad-ı Türki" (Pan-Turkism) based on racial identity with the influence of Akçura. Akçura believed that Muslims excluded from the Turkish identity would become Turkified through the establishment of a Turkish unity within the Ottoman Empire, which he saw as the largest and most civilized Turkish community. Akçura also discussed the romantic aspects of Turanism and believed that his "national ideal" of Turkish nationalism and Pan-Turkism was connected to the concepts of the "lost homeland" and living space. Ziya Gökalp, who linked the Turan ideal with the Ural-Altaic language family, emphasized that Turks were a part of the Islamic community. In the Turan ideal, religious affiliation was considered the primary basis. Turanists saw Anatolia as the second Ergenekon (mythical place of Turkic origin). With the withdrawal of the Ottoman Empire from Europe and the final destination of the Ottoman Turks being Anatolia after their withdrawal from Europe, Turkish nationalists, both before and after the Republic, attached special value to Anatolia. Many foreign intellectuals who were familiar with Turkey shared similar opinions. Karl Bernhard von Moltke and Arminius Vambéry believed that the Turks, by withdrawing from Europe to Asia, could create a great empire. They argued that an empire stretching from the Adriatic Sea to the Great Wall of China was possible. Similarly, considering the loss of Rumelia and the decreasing importance of trade routes, Goldziher Pasha mentioned during the Thessaloniki Campaign that Istanbul had lost its significance, suggesting that the capital could be moved to Anatolia. The ideas of these foreign intellectuals influenced defeated and discouraged Turkish intellectuals, giving them a new sense of purpose. Golt and Vambéry, who did not hesitate to regard Anatolia as a new Ergenekon, were particularly influential.

The Committee of Union and Progress

The Committee of Union and Progress (CUP), also known as the Ittihad ve Terakki Cemiyeti (Union and Progress Society), was founded in 1899 by four students in the form of a secret society. Its primary goal was to overthrow the authoritarian regime to save the empire from disintegration. The society was structured in a cell-like manner and operated as a clandestine organization. The name of the society changed several times. The overseas branch, which could engage in open activities and move more freely, was more effective.

In 1907, the committee merged with the Ottoman Freedom Society, founded by Talat Bey and his associates in 1906 in Thessaloniki, and adopted the name "Ittihad ve Terakki Cemiyeti" (CUP). Talat Bey, along with Mithat Şükrü, Rahmi Aslan, İsmail Canpolat, Ömer Naci, and Mehmet Tahir, had established the Ottoman Freedom Society.

As a result of the guerilla activities organized by the CUP in Macedonia in 1908, Sultan Abdulhamid declared the Second Constitutional Era on July 24, 1908. After the declaration of constitutionalism, a secret congress held in Thessaloniki decided to transform the society into a political party. In the elections held in December 1908, where both the CUP and the Ahrar Party participated, the CUP secured the majority in the parliament. Indeed, in February 1909, with the votes of party members, the Kamil Pasha government was overthrown, and the Hilmi Pasha government was formed. Although the CUP had a majority in the parliament, it did not form a government or appoint ministers but took on a supervisory role.

After the events of the 31st of March Incident, the CUP further strengthened its position by overthrowing Abdulhamid II and sending him into exile. In August 1909, a constitutional amendment shifted political power to the parliament, making the monarchy symbolic. The elections held in 1912, known in our democratic history as the "elections with cudgels," resulted in the victory of the CUP. In 1913, following the Babı Ali Incident organized by Enver Pasha, the CUP seized power entirely. The 1914 elections, held after the liberation of Edirne, also ended with the victory of the CUP. The party governed the country until its dissolution in 1918. Following the defeat in the war, party leaders went into exile. While Enver Pasha fought against the Soviets in Turkestan and became a martyr, other CUP leaders lost their lives due to assassinations. Those who remained in Istanbul officially dissolved the party on paper. The majority of the people held the CUP responsible for entering the war, losing the war, the hardships endured during the war, and the occupation by the enemy. Even the victorious Allies were angry with the CUP because they believed that the CUP had led the Ottoman Empire into the war. Therefore, the war, which was planned to be short, lasted much longer. The Allied forces had to open new fronts and suffered significant casualties, especially in the battles with the Ottomans at Çanakkale, Iraq, and Syria.

When the Committee of Union and Progress (CUP) was first established as a society in its early years, it consisted of individuals with different views who came together to oppose the authoritarian regime and demand the reopening of the parliament. There was no common view or program. The society included people from various backgrounds and beliefs. After the declaration of constitutionalism in 1908, a non-centralist wing advocating liberal views split from the CUP and founded the Ahrar Party. From 1908 onwards, the CUP began to advocate for the idea that the Ottoman Empire should be structured as a centralized and strong state model. It had a nationalist agenda, supported Westernization and modernization, and aimed to bring modern education to the remotest corners of the empire. Serving the state was of paramount importance. In the early years of the Committee, particularly until the Balkan Wars, Ottomanism was the dominant ideology. The goal was to keep the Ottoman Empire standing with a constitutional and parliamentary monarchy. However, after the Balkan Wars, the Turkish nationalist movement gained prominence within the CUP. Due to the multi-ethnic nature of the Ottoman Empire, Turkish nationalism was never prominently displayed. Ottomanism and the Unity of Islam were maintained in rhetoric and appearance. The removal of capitulations in the economy was sought. When World War I began, the CUP leaders declared that they had lifted all capitulations. During the CUP's rule, free enterprise and the private sector were supported, and national industry was protected and encouraged.

Nationalist Movement Party (MHP)

Many political analysts who discuss recent political history often connect the Nationalist Movement Party (MHP), the party of the Idealist Movement (Ülkücü Hareket), to either the Committee of Union and Progress (CUP), the People's Party (Millet Partisi), or the Republican People's Party (CHP). However, the Idealist Movement, developed by Alparslan Türkeş by drawing on the accumulated wisdom of the past, is an original ideological system. The MHP is the institutionalized form of the Idealist Movement. Türkeş did not first create the idea of "Ülkücülük" and then establish the MHP. Türkeş, as much an action-oriented figure as he was a thinker, matured both the party and the ideology simultaneously, with the ideology feeding the party and vice versa.

Those who link the Idealist Movement to the Committee of Union and Progress argue that the CUP represents the right-wing and the MHP, while the CHP represents the left-wing of the CUP. While the CUP, especially after the Balkan Wars, emphasized Turkish nationalism and expressed it loudly, it is essential to note that the CUP and the MHP were established in very different political contexts. The MHP is a party that values republicanism and democracy and attaches importance to legitimacy. The CUP was founded as a secret organization, primarily a group of conspirators advocating for monarchy and caliphate. Up until the day they came to power, or more accurately, overthrew Abdulhamid II, the CUP included people of all views, a kind of "Babel Tower." Those who joined the CUP shared the common goal of saving the country from collapse, which was heading towards destruction. In the following years, those CUP members who adopted Atatürk's nationalist, republican, and modernizing views joined the CHP. Others were purged from political life. What both the CUP and the Idealists share is their deep patriotism and sacrifice. The majority of both groups were heroes. The members of the CUP rushed to every corner of the Ottoman territory, even marching to their deaths without hesitation. After the defeat, they supported the National Liberation War led by Atatürk. The Idealists showed a similar approach during the period of 1970-1980. This is the most apparent similarity between the two groups. Türkeş, who created the Idealist Movement, criticized the adventurist CUP members heavily. He stated, "In our recent history, there is the Committee of Union and Progress (CUP). There are Enver, Talat, and Cemal Pashas. Many people admire them. They say they were very honest, upright people. Look, Enver Pasha left, he was martyred in Turkestan. But what's the use of it after they destroyed the great Ottoman State? The CUP came to power in 1908. When they came to power, Albania was a part of the Ottoman State. The borders of the Ottoman State extended to the Adriatic Sea. All of Rumelia was under our administration. Thessaloniki, Bitola, Niš, Kosovo, they were all under our rule. Libya and Chad were ours. In other words, one end of our border was in the middle of the Indian Ocean in 1908. After ten years, in 1918, they were all gone. The country was occupied in Anatolia. Anatolia was in danger. This is the Committee of Union and Progress. This is Enver Pasha. This is Talat Pasha. This is Cemal Pasha. Yes, they were very patriotic, very honest, not thieves, and so on. Yes, but they were conspirators. Conspirators and statesmanship are different things. We need statesmen who are intelligent, forward-thinking, who know their people, who know their history, and who are powerful." When Türkeş became the leader of the Idealists and the president of the Nationalist Movement Party (MHP), he was well-prepared. He demonstrated how prepared he was during his six-month tenure as the Undersecretary of the Prime Ministry.

The People's Party (Millet Partisi or MP) was founded on July 20, 1948, under the leadership of Fevzi Çakmak by deputies who had left the Democratic Party (DP). MP cadres accused the DP of conducting guided opposition. They argued that the DP should withdraw from the parliament and turn to the people directly, emphasizing that meaningful results could not be achieved without conducting opposition in the streets alongside the people. When Celal Bayar stated that he would never allow this, Fevzi Çakmak left the DP. The number of deputies who left the DP was greater than those who remained. MP favored a liberal economy. They advocated for a single-term presidency and a bicameral parliament. The party demanded the removal of the Six Arrows (altı ok) from the constitution and strongly criticized the CHP's approach to religion and secularism. After the death of Fevzi Çakmak, MP lost its influence, and in the 1950 elections, it only received 3.11% of the vote, resulting in the election of just one MP. In the 1952 Congress, there were internal debates within the party regarding the visit to Anıtkabir. Significant figures left the party. The party was closed by the court in 1954, citing its reliance on religious principles. MP expressed ideas similar to those of the Terakkiperver Fırka. Particularly after the death of Çakmak Pasha, MP shifted toward an anti-Atatürk line. It is incorrect to claim that the People's Party (MP) was the precursor of the MHP, as some political analysts suggest. The MHP has never been Kemalist or adherent to Atatürk's principles, but it has always respected Atatürk. It has regarded Atatürk as the nationalist leader who founded Turkey. Furthermore, the MHP is not liberal like the MP; it supports a mixed economy. The similarities between the two parties lie in their opposition to İsmet İnönü and their demand for a secularism that respects religious beliefs.

It is true that the Nationalist Movement Party (MHP) is formally considered the successor of the Republican People's Party (CHP) after its transformation. However, this transformation was merely formal. After the closure of the People's Party (Millet Partisi or MP), figures such as Osman Bölükbaşı, Enis Akaygen, Ahmet Tahtakılıç, and Hasan Koçdemir, who were originally from the People's Party, founded the Republican Peasants' People's Party (Cumhuriyetçi Köylü Millet Partisi or CKMP). In essence, the CKMP echoed the same ideas as the People's Party but soon turned into "Osman Bölükbaşı's party" and could not find success outside of Kırşehir. In October 1958, the CKMP merged with the Turkey Peasants' Party, which had failed to gain traction in the 1957 elections, and became the Republican Peasants' People's Party.

In the 1961 elections, the CKMP received 14% of the vote, coming in third place. It became one of the addresses for democrats opposed to the CHP. In 1962, it formed a coalition with the CHP. The CHP-AP coalition established after the 1961 elections had collapsed because the CHP did not support the Democrat Party members' amnesty requests presented by the AP. Bölükbaşı and his friends, who were against forming a coalition with the CHP but were in the minority, left the party and founded the People's Party (Millet Partisi). Bölükbaşı believed that a coalition that did not grant amnesty to DP members would consume the CKMP. After Bölükbaşı's departure and due in part to its entry into the coalition, the CKMP entered a period of decline. In the 1963 local elections, the party could only secure 3% of the vote.

In 1965, Türkeş, along with some former members of the Nationalist Movement Organization (MBK), joined the party and was elected as its leader in the same year. At the 1965 congress, Türkeş competed with Ahmet Tahtakılıç, who led those practicing the classic MP-CKMP line. When Türkeş won the election, the classic CKMP members left the party. Türkeş's sympathizers and young people began to join the party. With Türkeş becoming the General Chairman, the transformation of the CKMP into the MHP began. The Nine Lights, first read at the 1965 Congress, became part of the party's program at the 1967 Congress. The party, in the 1965 (2.2% of the vote and 9 deputies) and 1969 (3% of the vote and 1 deputy) elections, received similar percentages of votes as in the 1963 elections. In other words, Türkeş and his associates managed to halt the decline within the party but did not achieve a significant increase in votes.

The party's name was changed to MHP (Nationalist Movement Party) at the 1969 Adana Congress. Türkeş quickly turned the MHP into the center of Turkish nationalism ideology and its political representative. The MHP adopted a form of nationalism that centered around Islam. Slogans such as "Our Turkic body, our Islamic soul; a soulless body becomes a corpse," "Even if our blood flows, victory belongs to Islam," and "As Turkish as Mount Ararat, as Muslim as Mount Hira" exemplify this approach. In 1969, at the Party Congress, the MHP adopted the three crescents used by the Ottoman Empire as its emblem, with the Gray Wolf, the symbol of the Idealist Hearths (Ülkü Ocakları), within the three crescents.

In the 1973 elections, the MHP received approximately 3.4% of the vote, and in 1977, it experienced a surge in support, garnering 6.4% of the vote. In the 1979 by-elections, it slightly increased its votes to 6.6%.

Alparslan Türkeş

Alparslan Türkeş was born in 1917 in Nicosia. His family was originally from the Afshar Turks, who were exiled from Kayseri, Pınarbaşı, to Cyprus in 1860 by a decree of Sultan Abdulaziz. When Türkeş was born, World War I was ongoing, and Cyprus had been under British occupation since 1878. In 1917, Turkish and British armies were in a state of war. There had been bloody battles in places like Gallipoli, Iraq, and Syria-Palestine, with a significant loss of life, particularly among British soldiers. Therefore, for the Turkish Cypriots, who were living under British rule in Cyprus, the British were seen as the relatives of those who had killed their fellow countrymen. When World War I ended with Britain's victory, the British celebrated, while the Turks mourned and grieved. After the signing of the Armistice of Mudros, Anatolia and Thrace began to be occupied. As these occupations started, Turks naturally began to organize against them. In Cyprus, the Greeks, who gradually advanced from Izmir and occupied Anatolia step by step, supported the Turkish War of Independence. The major supporter of the Greek army's invasion of Anatolia was Britain. Thus, Cyprus was divided into two parts, with the majority Greeks and the British governing class on one side and the oppressed and marginalized Turks on the other. The defeat and expulsion of the Greek army from Anatolia, which led to the establishment of the Republic of Turkey, intensified the anti-Turkish sentiment among the Greek Cypriots. Türkeş spent his childhood and early youth in this environment. This environment greatly contributed to his strong sense of Turkish identity and his later advocacy of the Turan ideal, which called for the independence of captive Turks first and then the unification of all Turks. In 1933, he returned to the Turkish mainland with his family. He received military training and graduated as a second lieutenant in 1939. He served in various parts of the country and became known for his nationalist and Turanist ideas, as well as his opposition to the CHP (Republican People's Party) and İsmet

İnönü. Türkeş experienced severe torture during his imprisonment as part of the Racism and Turanism Trial in 1944, where he was accused of holding such beliefs. He and his companions were imprisoned for an extended period but were acquitted in 1947. The torture he endured in prison and the Boraltan Bridge incident, in which 195 Azerbaijani Turks were handed over to the Soviets and killed, further fueled Türkeş's opposition to İnönü and the CHP. Türkeş, from the moment he was established, had sympathies for the Democratic Party (DP). Prominent Turkish nationalists such as Hamdullah Suphi Tanrıöver, Sait Bilgiç, and Halide Edip Adıvar were in the DP. Türkeş went to the United States in 1948 to receive guerrilla warfare training. Upon his return, he initially provided guerrilla warfare training within the military. Later, he continued his education at the War Academy and graduated as a major. Following his graduation, he was assigned to the Pentagon by the DP government. Until 1958, he served as a permanent representative of Turkey at NATO headquarters in Washington, D.C. While in the United States, he also received training in international economics. In 1959, the DP government sent Türkeş to Germany to receive education at the Atomic and Nuclear School. After his return from Germany, he was appointed as a colonel and the Director of the NATO Branch within the Turkish Land Forces Command. Türkeş enjoyed support from the DP government and was promoted rapidly, not only because he received special training but also because he was considered a promising and talented officer. Between 1950 and 1955, during a period when only a limited number of officers received advanced training in guerrilla warfare, Türkeş was one of those who did. He managed the process of arming and training the mujahideen in Cyprus and provided similar support to the mujahideen in Algeria. During this period, Türkeş represented the military, while Fatin Rüştü Zorlu represented the Ministry of Foreign Affairs. Zorlu was close to both President Celal Bayar and Prime Minister Adnan Menderes. Therefore, Türkeş's nationalist, patriotic, diligent, and visionary qualities were emphasized repeatedly. Türkeş actively worked to prevent the coup led by Talat Aydemir on May 20, 1963, which ultimately failed. He informed his senator and deputy friends about the coup preparations through Reşat Akşemsettinoğlu, allowing necessary measures to be taken and thwarting the coup attempt. Some political commentators accuse Türkeş of being aligned with the United States and label him a "NATO man." They associate this with his involvement in the military coup on May 27.

However, if that were the case, he would not have been purged and sent into exile. Türkeş received extensive training in the United States and Germany because he passed the necessary exams and was a promising officer. Moreover, during the years when most of Turkish territory was occupied by the Soviet Union and China, with Turkey also under threat from the USSR, it was only logical to cooperate with NATO. During his political career, Türkeş did not follow a pro-American policy. He signed the decision to close American military bases and expel American military personnel from Turkey. He fully supported the Cyprus intervention and the continuation of opium cultivation policies. The trials of the September 12 coup, which was carried out with the guidance of the White House, kept Türkeş in detention for nearly five years and sentenced him to death. The MHP (Nationalist Movement Party) and the Idealist Hearths (Ülkü Ocakları) suffered the most during the oppression of the September 12 period. (In the 1970s, Paul Henze, the CIA's Ankara Chief, reported the September 12 coup to President Jimmy Carter by saying, "Our boys have done it.")

After Türkeş was released from prison, he fought for the removal of the ban on political activities imposed by the coup leaders on politicians before September 12. Ultranationalists appointed by Türkeş founded the Conservative Party in 1983. Due to the veto of the coup leaders and the pressures applied, the Conservative Party could not participate in the general elections in 1983 or the local elections in 1984. In 1985, the party's name was changed to the Nationalist Labor Party (MÇP) at the congress. In the by-elections held in 1986, the MÇP received 2.2% of the vote. When political bans were lifted by referendum in 1987, Türkeş was elected as the party's leader, and in the general elections of 1987, the MÇP received 3% of the vote. In the 1989 local elections, they received 4.2% of the vote. Türkeş was re-elected as a Member of Parliament in the 1991 elections from the Welfare Party (RP) list. After this period, especially following the dissolution of the Soviet Union and the independence of the Turkic republics, Türkeş focused on institutionalizing these newly independent states and improving relations with Turkey. He brought up numerous issues such as moving the capital of Kazakhstan to Astana, the Baku-Tbilisi-Ceyhan Oil Pipeline, and the Zangezur Corridor. Thanks to his close relationship with Süleyman Demirel, he played a role in the establishment of an autonomous republic for the Gagauz Turks and the return of the Crimean Turks to their homeland. He contributed to the formalization of the Crimean National Assembly as an official body. During this period, he engaged in numerous diplomatic contacts on behalf of Turkey, especially in managing the normalization of relations with Armenia. Türkeş passed away in 1997.

Alparslan Türkeş in Foreign Documents

In this section of our work, we will benefit from the information provided by Prof. Dr. Mehmet Akif Okur, who specializes in Turkish foreign policy and Turkish-American relations, based on his research in the national archives in the United States, as well as external archives and sources related to foreign affairs in 2014.

"The first document indicates that the Americans believed that immediately after May 27th, Türkeş took a 'neutral' stance against the DP and CHP. Istanbul Consul General Robert G. Miner's report to the Ministry of Foreign Affairs dated June 30, 1960, includes assessments of a private meeting he had with journalist Özcan Ergüder. It is stated here that Türkeş was not only against the DP but also against the CHP and İnönü, and he intended to lead a new party into the elections. This information provides explanatory clues about a contentious issue regarding May 27th. After the coup, there were attempts to explain Türkeş and his colleagues' reluctance to hold elections immediately and transfer power to civilians as anti-democratic and coup-oriented. However, holding elections right away in an environment where the DP was convicted would mean handing over power to the CHP with the help of the military. Türkeş and his colleagues were also opposed to the CHP. Therefore, they wanted the military government to remain in power for a while to allow new parties to be established and organized. In a national intelligence assessment prepared 20 days after Miner's report, statements about Türkeş's worldview are mentioned. While analyzing the general framework of the National Unity Committee (MBK), Türkeş is shown as the most influential member after Gürsel. The document also mentions that Türkeş was an ardent Turkish nationalist and that he was arrested in 1944 due to his Pan-Turanist ideas aimed at achieving the independence of Turks within the USSR. In Ambassador Warren's report to the Ministry of Foreign Affairs dated July 25, 1960, it is mentioned that a meeting was held with Gürsel, Türkeş, and Kuneralp regarding the credit requested by Turkey from the US. In this meeting, Türkeş indirectly threatened US officials by saying that some officers in the army needed the money urgently for their forced retirement and that if the US didn't provide the funds, they could find the money "from anywhere." In the end of the report, Warren states that any action plan prepared by Türkeş, focusing on the needs of the MBK and the reluctance of the US to meet these needs, would be unilateral and would not consider the US's position and obligations.

In a CIA daily intelligence note dated July 28, 1960, marked "Top Secret," similar points to those mentioned in Warren's letter are included. It is emphasized that Gürsel and Türkeş told US Ambassador Warren that they would take decisive action regarding the forced retirement of senior officers in the Turkish army even if American financial aid was not forthcoming and that they could find the money "from anywhere" if the US did not provide it. However, it is noted that although any step taken by Gürsel would not be a surprise, it was not expected that he would approach the USSR to obtain funds. Similar evaluations are not made for Türkeş. According to Warren, the MBK is composed of young, inexperienced, and patriotic officers. Türkeş, who is considered the most influential member of the Committee after Gürsel, is described as having "fanatic zeal, an inferiority complex, and deep emotions." It is also mentioned that in case of any division within the MBK, Türkeş is the only person who could potentially replace Gürsel. In a CIA daily intelligence note dated September 26, 1960, marked "Top Secret," Türkeş's resignation from the position of Undersecretary of the Prime Ministry on September 22 is evaluated. In the note, it is discussed that this event revealed the increasing conflict between the young, ambitious nationalist group and the larger conservative elements within the MBK, and that Major General Madanoğlu emerged as Türkeş's leading opponent. Türkeş's resignation is seen as exacerbating the unrest within the MBK. The document emphasizes the potential threat posed by Türkeş's "radical" group within the armed forces to the existing Western-oriented administration. Although the removal of the 14-member nationalist group under Türkeş's leadership is considered as a step supported by the stronger team within the MBK, it is noted that the "radical" group led by Türkeş is seen as a potential threat to the Western-oriented administration. The language of the report summarizes the main lines of the US approach to the cadre that carried out May 27th. According to this, the MBK was composed of Western-oriented individuals as well as nationalists led by Türkeş. The White House sympathized with the Western-oriented group rather than the radicals. As a result, the government remained in the hands of the group favored by Washington. When we look at the subsequent reports prepared by the CIA, we see how much the potential consequences of the removal of the 14 individuals were valued by the United States. In a weekly intelligence report dated November 17, 1960, it is stated that Türkeş, who is considered the spokesperson for young officers, will most likely continue his life as a political figure and will receive the support of the 3,500 officers who are forcibly retired from the military. The report also notes that any action taken by Gürsel will not be surprising, but it is not expected that he will approach the USSR to obtain funds. Similar assessments are not made for Türkeş. According to Warren, the MBK is composed of young, inexperienced, and patriotic officers. Türkeş, who is considered the most influential member of the Committee after Gürsel, is described as having "fanatic zeal, an inferiority complex, and deep emotions." It is also mentioned that in case of any division within the MBK, Türkeş is the only person who could potentially replace Gürsel. In a CIA daily intelligence note dated September 26, 1960, marked "Top Secret," Türkeş's resignation from the position of Undersecretary of the Prime Ministry on September 22 is evaluated. In the note, it is discussed that this event revealed the increasing conflict between the young, ambitious nationalist group and the larger conservative elements within the MBK, and that Major General Madanoğlu emerged as Türkeş's leading opponent. Türkeş's resignation is seen as exacerbating the unrest within the MBK. The document emphasizes the potential threat posed by Türkeş's "radical" group within the armed forces to the existing Western-oriented administration. Although the removal of the 14-member nationalist group under Türkeş's leadership is considered as a step supported by the stronger team within the MBK, it is noted that the "radical" group led by Türkeş is seen as a potential threat to the Western-oriented administration. The language of the report summarizes the main lines of the US approach to the cadre that carried out May 27th. According to this, the MBK was composed of Western-oriented individuals as well as nationalists led by Türkeş. The White House sympathized with the Western-oriented group rather than the radicals. As a result, the government remained in the hands of the group favored by Washington. When we look at the subsequent reports prepared

In the table of contents of the CIA's weekly propaganda guide dated December 5, 1960, there is a section related to the purge of the 14 members, titled "Difficult-to-Reconcile Members Removed by the Temporary Turkish Government." The document describes the removal of the 14 members, led by Türkeş, as an "obstinate and uncompromising group" from the National Unity Committee (MBK) and speculates on Türkeş's potential entry into politics. Furthermore, it suggests that with the removal of the 14 members who had previously shown tendencies towards an independent foreign policy, the possibility of a shift in Turkey's foreign policy axis had been eliminated, and thereby, the Gürsel government's commitment to the previously pursued pro-Western foreign policy was secured.

Continuing to trace the records in the archives, we see that the purging within the National Unity Committee and the subsequent exile did not alleviate the concerns of the United States regarding Türkeş. Approximately one and a half months before the 1961 elections, a letter from Ambassador Raymond A. Hare to Washington discusses the possibility of Türkeş and his team organizing a military intervention. Hare mentions in his letter that they know Türkeş's supporters within the military are mostly composed of low-ranking officers, but they are unsure about the extent of Türkeş's organization. He suggests that if unrest were to break out in Turkey after the elections, Türkeş could seize the opportunity for intervention, but if the chain of command were to act before him, this possibility would diminish.

The worried assessments of the potential moves by Türkeş and his colleagues in exile continued after the elections held on October 15, 1961. In a CIA weekly intelligence report dated November 17, 1961, which was over a month after the elections, it is noted that the failure to form a government had started causing problems nationwide and within the armed forces. The report suggests that especially if the unrest within the military were to escalate, Türkeş and the 14 members in exile might exert pressure for the continuation of military rule. The documents indicate that the United States continued to monitor Türkeş even after he entered politics following his years in exile. In a special report prepared by the CIA before the 1965 general elections, Türkeş is described as appearing to believe in Turkey's existing ties with the West but is actually inclined towards neutrality. In American archives, we also find records reflecting Türkeş's foreign policy perspective. For instance, a telegram sent by the U.S. diplomatic mission in June 1967 reporting on Turkey's stance during the increased tension between Israel and Arab states reveals that while the government and political leaders, including far-left groups, remained silent during the growing tension between Arabs and Israel, only Türkeş and Bölükbaşı took a pro-Arab stance.

When we examine documents from the 1970s, we see that there was no change in the negative attitude of the United States towards Türkeş during this period. An important document that reflects Washington's perspective is a CIA report dated January 1, 1973, regarding student uprisings in various countries. In this report, the CIA mentions that in Turkey, the youth had rapidly divided into two camps, one being the Marxist youth generally influenced by TİP, and the other being the "commando" youth led by Türkeş, described as "neo-fascist" and the leader of CKMP. The use of the term "fascist-neo-fascist," which is associated with Hitler and Mussolini and has a chilling effect in the West, to describe Türkeş is a significant indication of the U.S. view of the MHP leader. Moreover, such labels are repeated in various documents. For example, in a National Intelligence Bulletin dated April 1, 1975, which evaluates the MC Government formed during Demirel's prime ministry, it is suggested that Türkeş's presence in the coalition, as the leader of an "ultra-right" MHP with alleged 100,000 "commandos," could pose a problem for Demirel. The concern was that Türkeş and Erbakan's participation in the MC Government would exacerbate political polarization, as stated in a Weekly Intelligence Summary dated April 4, 1975. The report emphasizes that the involvement of Türkeş and Erbakan in the government would further intensify political polarization.

A CIA report dated June 20, 1975, reveals insights into how the United States viewed the escalating violence in Turkey. The report suggests that in order to gain public support for taking harsh measures, Demirel had to restrain both right-wing and left-wing groups. It also highlights that especially the "commandos" allegedly led by Türkeş needed to be suppressed. The concerned assessments by the U.S. regarding Türkeş's potential actions continued after the 1977 elections. In an Intelligence Bulletin dated January 31, 1976, it is suggested that Türkeş's supporters within the coalition government had involvement in the ongoing violence due to Demirel's inability to use his authority effectively. This view is reiterated in a National Intelligence Daily Cable dated November 2, 1976. However, in the following months, the relentless terror activity led to a more balanced evaluation of the situation, as seen in the National Intelligence Daily Cable dated August 10, 1977. The cable points out that urban left-wing terrorism was on the rise and that right-wing groups were being targeted not through random campus incidents but through planned assassinations. It also notes that in the face of these events, Türkeş, in his capacity as Deputy Prime Minister, maintained a calm and moderate stance. However, it is mentioned that if left-wing terrorism continues, the right-wing might respond, and Türkeş could adopt a tough stance against government actions that could influence his supporters.

The report titled "International Narcotics Review" dated January 19, 1978, also addresses the escalating terrorist incidents in Turkey. The report identifies the Turkey People's Liberation Army as the main center of violence on the left. It mentions that right-wing extremists are organized within the Idealist Hearths, which are ideologically protected under Türkeş's leadership in the Nationalist Movement Party (MHP). The report repeats the claim that Türkeş trained his fervent supporters known as "Grey Wolves" in paramilitary camps. However, it also suggests that Türkeş encouraged his "young warriors" not to engage in widespread confrontations with leftists to strengthen his political position. This approach might lead some fervent right-wing individuals to become less loyal to Türkeş and act independently. The United States closely monitored the steps taken by the Ecevit Government to close down the Idealist Hearths. In a Security National Intelligence Cable prepared on November 28, 1978, it is noted that the mutual accusations between Ecevit and Türkeş implied that if a ban were imposed on the idealists, Türkeş might respond. This situation could further worsen Turkey's fragile political landscape. Moreover, it is suggested in the intelligence report that if they were to face a ban, "radical rightists" might intensify their activities and even redirect their actions from leftists to government forces. It is also mentioned that in such a situation, commercial and political elites might pressure the Ecevit Government to declare martial law.

In a report prepared by the National Foreign Assessment Center of the CIA on December 27, 1978, Ecevit's accusations against Türkeş regarding the Maraş incidents are highlighted, emphasizing the possibility that they might turn out to be true. This is used to justify the government's prohibition of the youth movement of the "neo-fascist MHP."

In another National Intelligence Daily Cable dated January 4, 1979, the label that had become common in correspondences related to the MHP in Turkey is once again used. Türkeş, the leader of the "neo-fascist MHP," is accused of being behind the motivated right-wing violence in the country. His statement that the government and society were leaning towards communism is reported by the CIA with the qualification "alleged."

Even after the military coup of September 12, 1980, CIA documents show that there was no change in the perspective and descriptions used regarding Türkeş. For example, in an intelligence report dated February 22, 1982, it is mentioned that the policies of the Evren Administration's political cleansing targeted both "communists" and "fascists" led by Türkeş. In a CIA report on terrorist organizations in Turkey dated September 12, 1984, covering the period from the May 27 coup to after September 12, the Grey Wolves / Idealist Hearths are mentioned among various Marxist and Kurdish organizations. Türkeş, who leads this "neo-fascist" terrorist organization, is described as one of the key figures, and the organization's main goal is stated as Pan-Turanism, aimed at uniting countries with a Turkish majority. While the report indicates that Syria and Iran were supporting Marxist and Islamist groups in Turkey to sever Turkey's ties with the West and especially Israel, it does not mention any external support for the idealists.

The American documents covering the period from the May 27 coup to September 12, 1980, clearly demonstrate that Türkeş was one of the figures with whom the United States felt the most distant during the Cold War years. Türkeş's reflexes towards the Soviets did not lead to any change in the American perception of him. This picture provides clear answers to many questions that have puzzled a generation: The Idealist Movement, with its faults and merits, conducted its great struggle while firmly keeping its feet only on Turkish soil.

In an interesting coded message sent to Moscow by Russian officer Albert Valenski, who came to Turkey as an assistant military attaché in 1978, the following is mentioned: "Starting from Turkish nationalism, they aim to unite the countries with a Turkish majority under one roof. He tries to make them feel Turkish. Extremely dangerous..." This Russian officer, who served in Turkey from 1978 to 1980, returned in 1983 but was sent back to his country in 1984, being declared an unwanted person. WikiLeaks documents mention Türkeş as follows: "He is a Pan-Turkist. A staunch patriot. He consistently defended Turkey's interests at NATO Headquarters." The Communist Party's publication, Pravda, emphasizes Türkeş's close involvement with foreign Turks and describes him as a dangerous politician. In British intelligence documents, Türkeş is described as "A suspicious personality. A poor speaker but has the charm of being a man of conviction." In a report from the British Embassy in Ankara dated June 25, 1960, the British Ambassador summarizes, "The Prime Minister's Undersecretary, who was born in Cyprus, keeps a close eye on Cyprus and follows it closely."

Nine Lights (Dokuz Işık)

When Türkeş returned to his homeland from New Delhi, he decided to enter politics. While in New Delhi, he prepared a draft of his doctrine known as the "Nine Lights of Idealism." Upon his return, he refined the Nine Lights doctrine by consulting with prominent figures such as Atsız, Mümtaz Turhan, Erol Güngör, and Dündar Taşer. Hüseyin Nihal Atsız, who shared his ideas primarily with young people through publications like Atsız Mecmua, Orhun Dergisi, and Ötüken Dergisi, described the nation as a mature, organized community, and nationalism as a noble belief that requires sacrifice. Atsız considered Turkish nationalism and Turkish patriotism to be synonymous and referred to them as "ideals." He believed that a society without ideals is destined to become weak, oppressed, or even extinct. Those who believe in Turkish nationalism act not to elevate themselves but to elevate their nation. They prioritize national interests over personal interests and are characterized by morality, respect for their heritage, and loyalty to national values.

Atsız emphasized the importance of solidarity among Turkish nationalists to prevent internal disputes. He asserted that Turkish nationalists, whom he described as the sacrifices of the Turkish nation, should work tirelessly with an unwavering sense of duty, regardless of their roles. Atsız also advised against hypocrisy, sycophancy, rudeness, discourtesy, and inferiority complexes among Turkish nationalists. He believed that to become a global power, having a powerful language was essential, and this language should be used effectively in science and literature.

Atsız referred to the national consciousness, which he described as the awareness of the nation itself, as a guiding light that illuminates the homeland. He supported the idea of Turanism, aiming for the unification of Turks. Mümtaz Turhan, another contributor to Turkish nationalism, emphasized the importance of obtaining or producing scientific knowledge correctly. Turhan argued that Turkey's main cause was becoming a nation and acquiring a national culture, with nationalism being a means to achieve this primary goal. He emphasized that the national consciousness of the Turkish people should be based on science and morality, advocating for scientific nationalism.

Focusing extensively on culture, Turhan highlighted that language, religion, customs, habits, traditions, shared memories, and history were components of culture and the foundations of nationalism. He discussed the role of nationalism in the process of becoming a nation and acquiring a national culture, underlining its importance. Dündar Taşer, known for his vision of a Greater Turkey, considered any place with a Turkish majority, where the Turkish flag flew, as a homeland. He described those who could collectively exhibit the same reflexes, shaped by intense historical events and social life, in different geographies as a community. He believed that the goal of the Nationalist Movement was to restore the elements that defined the nation's true essence by removing foreign influences.

Taşer emphasized the need for an action-oriented movement that would gather the youth around ideals and ideas, considering the youth as the guarantor of the Turkish nation's future. He advocated for a youth that was free from foreign ideologies, emphasized spiritual and national values, and worked diligently to achieve this. Taşer believed that an action-oriented movement needed to be established to instill the concept of a Greater Turkey in the youth. He worked to construct and establish an anti-imperialist, nationalist, and spiritual thought system.

Erol Güngör, who contributed significantly to the theoretical structure of Turkish nationalism, viewed nationalism as closely tied to populism and democracy, emphasizing the importance of these two components. Güngör defined the goal of nationalism as establishing an independent political will based on the majority's consent and creating a national culture within that political unity. He saw nationalism as a means to achieve Turkey's main cause, which he identified as becoming a nation and acquiring a national culture. Güngör believed that the national consciousness of the Turkish people should be grounded in science and morality, advocating for scientific nationalism.

Güngör, in particular, underlined the importance of a strong language for a nation to become a global power, asserting that the language must be used effectively in science and literature. He described nationalism as a civilizational cause and refuted claims that it was akin to Nazism or fascism, emphasizing that it was not against religion. Güngör regarded nationalism as a movement rooted in history and society and not a superficial ideology. He believed that nationalism initially emerged as a political independence movement and later transformed into a cultural movement. Güngör regarded nationalism as a modernization ideology that aimed to create spiritual bonds between the past and future of a nation and highlighted the historical and sociological connection between democracy and nationalism.

The Nine Lights (Dokuz Işık) were included in the CKMP (Confederation of Turkish Nationalists) program in 1967. Nationalism, Idealism, Moralism, Science, Villagism, Communalism, Freedom, Individualism, Development, and Populism are the main principles of the

Nine Lights doctrine. This marked the first time a leader sought power with a detailed doctrine. Unlike center-right parties, which primarily followed a service-oriented policy, they were nationalist and conservative, but they had not transformed these beliefs into a doctrine, plan, or program. We know that Atatürk had a plan for what he would do when he founded the republic or when he landed in Samsun. He certainly had a plan for step-by-step implementation. However, because this plan was not shared with the public or made public, we do not know how much of it was implemented, what was left incomplete, or why certain things were abandoned. After Atatürk, the CHP (Republican People's Party) up until Ecevit remained disconnected from the public. The Six Arrows (Altı Ok) were repeatedly used as slogans. Ecevit first used the term "Center-Left" (Ortanın Solu) in 1965. He wrote articles and gave lectures on this topic, responding to criticisms. Over time, the "Center-Left" ideology matured and was documented in books. Despite becoming Prime Minister multiple times, it cannot be said that Ecevit took significant steps related to the Center-Left ideology.

The leaders of the Committee of Union and Progress (Ittihat ve Terakki), when they seized power through a coup, were unprepared for governance. They were very young and inexperienced. They believed that everything would improve once constitutionalism was established. When this did not happen, they thought that everything would improve once Abdulhamid was overthrown. After the coup, there was not a single minister from the Committee of Union and Progress in the cabinet. One of the most significant differences between the Nationalist Movement and the Ittihatçıs (Committee of Union and Progress) was this. Türkeş was prepared for power long before becoming the party leader. During his six-month tenure as the Undersecretary of the Prime Ministry, he was ready. He established critical institutions one after another during this short period, playing the most crucial roles in Turkey's development. Each of these institutions filled significant gaps and addressed deficiencies. For example, during the Democratic Party's (DP) era, Turkey experienced a successful development initiative. However, this initiative was not undertaken as a collective and long-term plan. The State Planning Organization (DPT) filled this gap. Investors were directed toward areas that were important and urgent for the country's development. When the automotive industry was established, the production of spare parts was also encouraged to minimize the sector's dependence on imports. During the DP era, there were significant gaps in all sectors, so the absence of an institution to plan and coordinate investments was not very noticeable. However, if the DPT had not been established, such successful results could not have been achieved in the following half-century. There would have been overcapacity or unprofitable investments in some sectors, and some sectors would have become entirely dependent on imports. The country's exports would have been lower, and imports would have been higher.

In his book "Yeni Ufuklara Doğru" (Towards New Horizons), Türkeş made the following assessments regarding the Nine Lights: "The Turkish nation, taking into account its national history, customs, traditions, and characteristics, should establish a fully native and national administrative system that leads modern science and technology. Because every nation's administrative system should be in line with its own conditions, preferences, and national characteristics. Taking another nation's system as it is does not conform to reality. Scholars are trying to implement capitalist and communist systems exactly as they are. All of these are imitations. Considering that each nation's situation is different, we say that a new national doctrine, a new system, is necessary. This doctrine is the Nine Lights."

"This national doctrine is based on everything that has been taken from Turkish history, embracing modern science and technology as leading factors. Its strength comes from its fundamental sources, which are Islam and Turkishness. Why are Islam and Turkishness the fundamental sources? Because this nation is the Muslim Turkish nation. For thousands of years, the Turkish people have a glorious history and honor. They have embraced Islam for a thousand years. In the last 50-60 years, intellectuals have opposed religion, not recognized Islam, and depicted it as harmful. They say that Europe advanced because it is Christian and that we lagged behind because we are Muslim. This is not true. The reason for our backwardness has nothing to do with religion. If it does, it is because some religious leaders have given wrong teachings. Islam is the most perfect religion. It values knowledge, contributes to the advancement of science and technology. Civilization in the Middle Ages was established thanks to Muslims in the East. The civilization was the Islamic Civilization. Today's European Civilization is not based on

Christianity or the Roman and Greek civilizations but on the Turkish-Islamic Civilization."

"Today, as acknowledged by many Western scholars, the foundation of Western Civilization is not ancient Greece, ancient Rome, or Christianity; it is the Turkish-Islamic Civilization. How did this happen? During the height of the Turkish-Islamic Civilization, Crusader armies entered Muslim lands. Europe was amazed when it saw this great civilization, and when the armies returned, they were inspired by it. The Crusades lasted for centuries."

"Many European scholars received education in mathematics, al-jabr (algebra), astronomy, and other sciences in Al-Andalus (Islamic Spain) during the reign of the Umayyads. They learned from Muslims. It is a well-known fact that, after the fall of the Umayyad state in Spain, Europeans plundered the books of science, and these books are now found in European libraries. Many Muslim Turkish scholars made significant discoveries. Finally, with the conquest of Istanbul by Mehmed the Conqueror, knowledge moved to Europe. Scholars who left Istanbul spread Islamic thought, explained its greatness, and inspired the Renaissance in Europe. It is clear that the advancement of Europeans is due to this great civilization. When scholars who did not grasp its main issues produced young, imitative intellectuals, we lagged behind."

"In other words, the main sources of the Nine Lights are as follows: Turkish consciousness, Islamic faith, Islamic ethics, and virtues. Another source is the love for humanity and boundless respect for human dignity. As the Turkish people, our national character has a distinct feature. We neither accept servitude to others nor use others as servants. We are against the mentality that does not respect human dignity, does not carry love for the Turkish people and the Turkish nation in their hearts, and looks down upon them. As Dokuz Işık adherents, we consider the Turkish people and Turkish individuals as a sacred trust from God. It is up to the administrators and intellectuals to serve all members of our nation in this understanding, regardless of their position, without taking into account differences in status or wealth. This depends on whether their hearts are filled with love for humanity and boundless respect for human dignity."

Türkeş, in Dokuz Işık (Nine Lights), defines nationalism as follows: "Nationalism, or idealism, is a term synonymous with the word 'idealism' borrowed from Western languages. Nationalism or idealism means conceiving and forming the most perfect, beautiful, and satisfying goals within the human mind, showing a desire for these goals to be achieved, and working towards their realization." He believes that societies and humanity as a whole need idealists or nationalists, stating, "Without idealists among people, humanity would not have achieved many of the developments and advancements that illuminate the world today. Every reality and every idea is born first as a dream in the minds of people. Nationalism, or idealism, is the process of conceiving and shaping such dreams within the human mind. In every society, there are idealists, nationalists, and their presence is a blessing for societies; it is a great fortune!"

Türkeş goes on to outline the framework of nationalism. He states, "Is this all that is within the boundaries of Turkish nationalism and idealism? Not only these but also other thoughts, other goals exist. These goals include the Turkish nation becoming a self-sufficient entity that does not beg for mercy from anyone, an entity that stands on its own strength, that preserves its existence by its own power and makes its voice heard everywhere in the world. In addition to this, it is the thought that the Turkish nation should always be able to introduce its rights to the world, make them known to the world, and, in line with the sacred principle of 'Self Determination,' all Turks should become independent, free from living under foreign rule, and each should become independent. These are some of the significant components of the ideal that a Turkish nationalist would think of for the Turkish society."

Later in the text, Türkeş elaborates on the concept of ideals, describing them as distant, long-term goals. He emphasizes that an ideal may not be realized immediately but serves as a guiding light for individuals. He states, "Ideals are far-reaching and long-term. An ideal may not be realized immediately. Ideals can cover the coming years, even centuries. However, an ideal is a light that illuminates the hearts of people. An ideal is a guide that determines the direction for people. For nations, a national ideal is the sun that illuminates the path of the nation. A person without ideals is like a creature made of mud. A person without ideals is like a ship without a rudder, like a ship without a compass. Therefore, every Turkish nationalist, every follower of the Nine Lights doctrine, will undoubtedly be an idealist; they will have an ideal. They will not only have a national ideal but also a humanistic ideal. They will have an ideal related to their own profession, so that they can develop as successful and beneficial individuals in their own profession and, at the same time, define and pursue their idealism related to their field in line with the fundamental and general principles of nationalism."

In the concluding section of his writing, Türkeş answers the question, "What is our nationalism?" by stating, "What is our nationalism? Our nationalism is to elevate the Turkish nation to the highest level of modern civilization in the shortest time, to make it happy and prosperous, to make it a free and self-reliant entity, and to work diligently and sacrificially for the advancement of the Turkish nation and the Turkish state, with unwavering loyalty. The greatest and most valuable investment is made in people. An idealistic, moral, and patriotic youth is the guarantee of the future of that nation."

Türkeş also emphasizes the importance of using reason and logic in all endeavors and highlights that Turkish nationalism is deeply rooted in history. He defines nationalism as a worldview and a thought system, where reason, common sense, justice, and intellect play crucial roles, and where the love for the Turkish nation and the desire to serve it are paramount. Türkeş insists that all actions must be in line with the Turkish spirit and tradition and that striving for the benefit of the Turkish people should be the foremost consideration. He also rejects all forms of racism, exclusivity, and intolerance, promoting a democratic system that values freedom, equality, and scientific thinking.

Türkeş's perspective on nationalism is firmly grounded in democratic principles, freedom, equality, inclusivity, and a commitment to serving the Turkish nation and humanity as a whole.

Türkeş defined the concept of a nation as a conscious community of people who share distinguishing characteristics such as a common language, heritage, ideology, culture, and history, independently existing with an awareness of living together. He believed that the Turkish people had been in the process of nation-building and state formation since ancient times. Türkeş regarded the emergence of nationalism in written history as evidenced by the resistance of Çi-Çi against Chinese captivity in the Great Hun Empire. German scholar Hirth once said, "In history, the first statesman who laid the foundation for nationalism in state politics is Çi-Çi." Türkeş emphasized that from the time of the Göktürk ruler Bilge Kağan onwards, the concept of nationalism was systematically implemented as state policy in Turkish states. However, he also noted that after the Turkish people embraced Islam, they did not fully utilize this concept, mainly because the term "nation" was associated with religion in Islamic terminology. Furthermore, as the spread of Islamic beliefs occurred through Arab and Persian cultures, Arab and Persian nationalism was actively promoted, while the use of Turkish nationalism or the term "Turk" was considered religiously problematic.

The concept of "millet" in Islamic context primarily referred to religious identity, which limited its secular use. Türkeş was aware of the religious boundaries of the term "millet" in Islam and the fact that it was mostly associated with religious identity. Additionally, he acknowledged that Arab and Persian nationalism had actively spread through the promotion of Islamic beliefs, whereas Turkish nationalism had not been emphasized as much due to religious sensitivities and historical factors.

The "Nine Lights" program, developed by Türkeş, was frequently referred to by members of the Nationalist Movement Party (MHP) before 1980 and served as a central reference point when seeking the support of voters. However, after 1980, its influence gradually declined, which is a natural development. Türkeş initially formulated the Nine Lights to address the problems of Turkey in the 1960s and 1970s. The world and Turkey in the 2000s were vastly different, so the MHP adapted its political strategies to the changing circumstances while remaining loyal to the core principles outlined in the Nine Lights.

The Nationalist Movement's Understanding of Nationalism

While Atatürk was institutionalizing the republic, he embraced Gökalp's culture-based nationalism concept. The phrase "Ne mutlu Türk'üm diyene!" (How happy is the one who says 'I am Turkish!') perfectly encapsulates this concept. It was not stated as "Ne mutlu Türk doğana" (How happy is the one born Turkish) or "Ne mutlu Türk olana" (How happy is the one who becomes Turkish). With the expression "Ne mutlu Türk'üm diyene," anyone who identifies as Turkish is considered Turkish. In practice, even non-Muslims who spoke Turkish, like the Karamanlı Turks, were included in the population exchange with Greece, despite being Turkish and expressing their Turkish identity. Pope Eftimin, the religious leader of the Karamanlı Turks, supported the National Struggle, was a friend of Mustafa Kemal Atatürk, and held nationalist views, yet this decision was made. During the population exchange, Muslims, including some Gypsies who didn't even speak Turkish, were accepted. Türkeş, after joining the CKMP (Nationalist Movement Party), attracted Turkish nationalists from various backgrounds and factions to the party. Nationalists of different views and factions united within the CKMP. The largest groups included the ethnic nationalists led by Atsız, the social nationalist groups clustered around former military personnel, and the conservative nationalists, including Osman Turan and Osman Yüksel Serdengeçti. Türkeş, with his Nine Lights doctrine, aimed to popularize an understanding that could integrate with the nation and solve Turkey's problems in the atmosphere of the 1960s and 1970s. Ahmet Arvasi played a significant role in the ideological development of the Nationalist Movement during this period, promoting the synthesis of Islam and Turkish nationalism. Seyit Ahmet Arvasi was born in 1932 in Van, Turkey, and like Gökalp, he was of Kurdish origin but considered himself Turkish. He graduated from the Pedagogy department of Gazi Education Institute in 1958. In 1966, he met Alparslan Türkeş and joined the CKMP. His 1967 book "Kendini Arayan Adam" (The Man Searching for Himself) gained recognition among young people. While continuing his career as a teacher, he started writing columns in the MHP's weekly newspaper in 1976, titled "Arada Bir Sohbet" (Occasional Conversations). Starting from 1978, he wrote a column named "Türk-İslam Ülküsü" (Turkish-Islamic Ideal) in the Hergün newspaper. His writings had a significant influence on the nationalist youth in the 1970s. Arvasi's teachings, particularly the "Turkish-Islamic Ideal," resonated with the socio-economic characteristics of the Nationalist Movement's youth base in the second half of the 1970s. This period witnessed rapid growth in the movement, with an increased presence of conservative, religiously inclined young people from rural areas and urban peripheries. Arvasi emphasized the need to reconnect the nation's youth with their national history, culture, and sacred values. He argued that through the Muslim Brotherhood movement, a plot was being hatched to erase both Turkish and Islamic nationalism, leaving nations defenseless. Arvasi saw attempts to create divisions between Turkish and Islamic fronts as treacherous. He defended the unity of Turkish-Islamic civilization, the Turkish-Islamic ideal, and the culture, ethics, faith, and love inherent in it. Arvasi considered nationalism as a natural state of being and stressed that Turkish nationalism drew strength from both science and its own history, economy, law, and psychological approaches. He believed that Turkish nationalism was not an ideology but an ideal, and it was rooted in the Turkish language, character, and ethics. He opposed Ibrahim Kafesoğlu's use of the term "synthesis" and instead introduced the term "ideal" to describe his concept. He emphasized that Turkishness and Islam were not antithetical; rather, they were complementary aspects of the same identity. After the military coup on September 12, 1980, Arvasi was arrested and became one of the defendants in the MHP's main trial but was released shortly after on January 9, 1981. After the coup, he continued to write columns for newspapers such as Yeni Düşünce and Türkiye. Unfortunately, Arvasi passed away in 1988 due to a heart attack.

During this period, influential intellectuals like Necmettin Hacıeminoğlu argued that nationalism was not merely a reactionary movement against opposing ideas or the antithesis of certain theses. Instead, he emphasized that nationalism was a thought system, not just a doctrine or a tool. Hacıeminoğlu asserted that nationalism was the ideal of preserving and elevating the Turkish nation along with its values for eternity. He believed that nationalism had existed among the Turks since their earliest known history and was rooted in knowledge, culture, and emotions.

Although considered conservative, Hacıeminoğlu described nationalism as open to innovation and development. He stressed that a genuine Turkish nationalist should sincerely embrace Turkish identity, feel Turkish, and take pride in being Turkish. He believed that Turkish nationalists should have a sense of Turkish pride and consciousness.

Galip Erdem, a senior figure among the nationalists, emphasized that Turkish nationalism did not discriminate based on religion, language, or ethnicity, highlighting that those who came together with love symbolized unity and solidarity. Galip Erdem regarded Turkish nationalism as contemporaneous with Turkish history and contributed to its evolutionary process, even though it may not have been fully theorized.

In the 1969 Congress, a final confrontation occurred between the supporters of Atsız, who advocated ethnic nationalism, and Türkeş, the leader of the Ülkücü movement. The Ülkücüler won the congress, and the Türkçüler left the party. Atsız summarized the congress by saying, "God has expelled God." Atsız's uniqueness was reflected in his mythological novels and poems. He wrote historical-mythological novels that recounted the adventures of heroic Turks in Central Asia with the aim of fostering national consciousness. These novels, known as the "Bozkurtlar series," were read by young generations and continue to be read today. Thanks to these novels, tens of thousands of young people became Ülkücüs

(Idealists) and continue to do so. Despite being a great writer and thinker, Atsız was not a politician, and his nationalist ideology remained on the margins of mainstream politics. His exclusionary stance, particularly towards Kurds, posed a significant challenge to national unity.

Devlet Bahçeli

Devlet Bahçeli was born in 1948 in Osmaniye, Turkey, into a large Turkish family known as the Fettahoğulları in the region. He received his primary education in Osmaniye and completed his secondary education in Istanbul. Bahçeli pursued his university education at the Ankara Academy of Economic and Commercial Sciences. From the beginning, he actively engaged in various roles within the Ülkücü Movement, dedicating himself to the cause.

In 1967, while still a student at the Ankara Academy of Economic and Commercial Sciences, Bahçeli took on the role of founder and leader of the Idealist Hearths (Ülkü Ocakları). He served as the General Secretary of the Turkish National Students' Federation (Türkiye Milli Talebe Federasyonu) from 1970 to 1971.

While actively participating in the Ülkücü Movement, Bahçeli continued his academic pursuits. Starting in 1972, he worked as an assistant in the Department of Economics at the Ankara Academy of Economic and Commercial Sciences. Bahçeli was a founding member of organizations such as the Association of Idealist Economists and Finance Experts (Ülkücü Maliyeciler ve İktisatçılar Derneği - ÜMİD-BİR) and the Association of University Academics and Assistant Professors (Üniversite Akademileri ve Yüksekokulları Asistanları Derneği - ÜNAY), where he also served as their chairman.

Devlet Bahçeli earned his doctoral degree in Economics from Gazi University's Institute of Social Sciences and worked as a faculty member in the Department of Economic Policy at the Faculty of Economics and Administrative Sciences at the same university until 1987. During this time, he conducted research in various fields, including Turkish-Islamic affairs, the Turkish economy, Turkish history, and foreign policy.

Following the coup on September 12, 1980, when many Ülkücüs were imprisoned, Bahçeli, along with Galip Erdem, took on a leadership role in advocating for the just causes of those incarcerated.

Devlet Bahçeli played a significant role in the training and development of Ülkücü cadres. When called upon by Alparslan Türkeş, he resigned from his university position and joined the ranks of the Nationalist Movement Party (Milliyetçi Hareket Partisi - MHP).

In the extraordinary congress held on April 19, 1987, Bahçeli was elected to the party leadership and appointed as the General Secretary of MHP. He held the position of General Secretary until 1993. Although he ran as a parliamentary candidate in the 1991 and 1995 elections, he was not successful in winning a seat. His role within MÇP and MHP's leadership has continued uninterrupted to the present day.

Devlet Bahçeli served in various positions within the party, including General Secretary, Deputy Chairman, Central Executive Board Member, Central Decision Board Member, and Chief Advisor to the Chairman. He was elected as the Chairman of MHP on July 6, 1997, during the 5th Extraordinary Congress.

He has been elected as a Member of Parliament (MP) for Osmaniye in the 21st, 23rd, 24th, 25th, 26th, and 27th legislative periods. In the 57th government, he held the positions of State Minister and Deputy Prime Minister.

C-) THE CODES OF THE NATIONALIST MOVEMENT

a) To Be Anti-Imperialist

The Nationalist Movement has always been inclined towards establishing dialogues with other countries and improving relations, regardless of distinctions like regime, system, or ideology. Turkey's place is within the Western Bloc. Turkey being part of the Western Bloc does not imply that it cannot pursue an independent foreign policy. Turkey is not and should not be a colony. Nationalists have argued that, when it comes to national interests, there should be no hesitation in engaging with allied states and superpowers, even if it means paying a price.

For instance, during Süleyman Demirel's term as Prime Minister, heavy industrial facilities like the Seydişehir Aluminum Plant and İskenderun Iron and Steel Factories were established with Soviet technology and credit. Demirel resisted the pressures from the United States regarding the ban on opium cultivation. In this struggle, MHP supported Demirel. When the United States imposed an embargo due to the Cyprus landing, the cabinet with Demirel as Prime Minister and Türkeş as Deputy Prime Minister closed military bases and deported American personnel. MHP, as an opposition party, provided full support for the Cyprus landing carried out by the CHP-MSP government.

Similarly, when Bülent Ecevit came to power in 1973 and allowed opium cultivation, Türkeş stood by Ecevit. The governments in which MHP was a partner resisted all pressures and did not allow Greece to return to NATO. Those who were susceptible to imperialist influence and conceded to demands were typically coup plotters and transitional governments during coup periods. Those who staged coups with claims like "the homeland is in danger" promptly complied with the desired concessions. Those like Türkeş, who defended the interests of the country, were purged within six months of the May 27th Revolution.

b) Staying Legitimate

The Nationalist Movement always adhered to laws and the existing legal system. It did not take to the streets or engage in mass protests. Prior to the military coup of September 12, the idealist youths, as they are known, defended themselves and their country against the communists who sought to turn Turkey into a Soviet satellite. Even during that time, the Central Office of the MHP made efforts to prevent confrontations. Measures such as temporarily closing the Central Youth Organization or local and provincial branches in areas where incidents escalated were taken to prevent events. After September 12, many idealist youths wanted to arm themselves and fight against PKK terrorism. The MHP leadership never allowed this. Idealists had no conflicts with either the PKK or HDP, which is the political wing of the PKK.

The Idealist Movement is not correctly understood in Western public opinion. The main reason for this is the bitter experiences Europeans had in the past. Hitler and Mussolini came to power democratically by establishing political parties, but after coming to power, they embraced fascism by putting democracy on the shelf. Both Hitler's Nazi Party and Mussolini's Fascist Party had civilian, armed youth organizations. Franco in Spain and Salazar in Portugal also used similar methods. Europeans think that idealists are like these fascist movements. They liken Idealist Youth Organizations to the SS and Blackshirts. This is a great misconception. First of all, Idealist Youth Organizations are not armed organizations. The only similarity with the others is that they are composed of young people. Idealist Youth Organizations recruit high school-aged youth, instill them with love for their homeland and nation, encourage them to read books, give seminars, and participate in debates. Through organized trips within the country, these young people get to know their homeland better. Idealist Youth Organizations educate and support underprivileged and impoverished children, provide them with an education, and make them useful members of society. Thanks to Idealist Youth Organizations, children from marginalized and poor backgrounds learn to love their country and feel a sense of ownership. Although Idealist Youth Organizations are a nationwide organization of young people, they have never been involved in any street incidents with the PKK, which has been bleeding Turkey for forty years. Can there be a better example to prove that the Idealist Movement is not an armed, destructive organization? The reason why Westerners liken idealists to armed organizations like the SS and Blackshirts is the struggle that was waged before 1980. However, the SS and Blackshirts were used by the Nazi Party and the Fascist Party to destroy the democratic order. The Nazis and fascists were theoretically opposed to democracy. On the other hand, the MHP has never been against democracy. On the contrary, it supported the institutionalization of democracy. The MHP lost the elections in 1965, 1969, 1973, and 1977. They accepted defeat gracefully and did not resort to other means. Before 1980, they came to power as a coalition partner after the elections. When they lost this position again in the elections, they handed over power within the framework of democratic rules. Idealists have never aimed to take over the state or destroy the democratic order. Before 1980, idealists waged an armed struggle, but they did so against terrorists who aimed to destroy the regime and establish a communist regime. If this struggle had not taken place, everything could have been different. The efforts of the communists to destroy Turkey had reached dangerous levels. After the danger was averted, idealists never took up arms again. Therefore, idealists are advocates of legitimacy. They participated in elections multiple times, gracefully accepted the results, came to power through elections, and left power through elections.

c) To be Anti-Communist

Nationalists are anti-communists. The nationalist stance against communism began in the 1930s. The main reason for this stance was the captivity of millions of Turks in the USSR and the colonization of Turkish lands. During the same period, Stalin, albeit implicitly, made demands, especially regarding the Turkish Straits, which also disturbed nationalists. There were significant contradictions between the worldview of nationalists and communism. However, if it weren't for these two issues, communism would not have been the primary enemy of Ülkücüs. After World War II, Stalin's termination of the Friendship Agreement between Turkey and the USSR, his demands regarding the administration of the Straits, and his desire for Kars and its surroundings, made the Soviets a primary threat to Turkey and nationalists. Turkey turned to NATO, and nationalists supported this shift. Furthermore, Bulgaria, Romania, Yugoslavia, and Albania had adopted communist regimes, so Turkey felt surrounded. The Soviet threat was very serious. The Red Army had occupied the Baltics, Eastern Europe, and the Balkans, establishing satellite regimes. They had incited civil war in Greece. They had occupied parts of Iran and North Korea. In 1949, the USSR became the second country to develop an atomic bomb. In 1951, Mao declared victory in China and transitioned to a communist system. In short, Turkey was under serious threat. Nationalists or those who governed Turkey did not turn to the United States because they were infatuated with it. They turned to it because there was no other choice. About 80% of the captive Turks were citizens of communist states. With each passing year, the number of pro-Soviet regimes increased, increasing Turkey's unease. Countries like Egypt, Iraq, Yemen, and Libya saw monarchies toppled and pro-Soviet regimes established. Even countries that gained independence, such as Algeria, Tunisia, and Syria, naturally leaned towards the USSR. If communism were to fall, and indeed it did, both the threat to Turkey and the freedom of captive Turks would be eliminated. We know that Türkeş and Atatürk had foreseen the collapse of the USSR. Türkeş had said the following during the Turancılar Trial, which began in 1944: "We are nationalists. We want all Turks, including those living in the world, to be happy, to be free from captivity. In other words, we carry this idea, if it's Turanism; we carry this idea. We are against communism. Communism is an ideological, political, and economic view that we do not like. We accepted writing nationalist articles, contributing to the country. That's why I sent articles to the Orkun Journal. I corresponded with Nihal Atsız from time to time about national issues." Türkeş's statements during the trial about future possibilities and predictions are noteworthy: "In my opinion, the most important thing is to work for everything to reach the highest level in every field. Turan, that is, the Turkish Unity, includes not only those in Asia but all Turks. In other words, the Turkish Unity includes not only those in Asia but also those in Bulgaria, Greece, and other places. Türkeş also pointed out that the Soviet Union could collapse, and Turanist movements could gain momentum, indicating that Russian and British-occupied Turkish territories could be liberated. "Today, just as in 1917, in 1965 or 1999, a revolution may occur in Russia. By that time, Turkey will have advanced in terms of defense industry, knowledge, and wisdom, and progress will be made towards this unity with Turkey's support. This is the opportunity." 58 years after Atatürk's speech and 47 years after Türkeş's speech, the Soviet Union collapsed. The Turkic Republics gained their independence. The struggles of nationalists from 1970 to 1980 and Afghan Mujahideen from 1979 to 1989 were decisive in the collapse of the Soviet Union. If Turkey had become communist, the USSR would have gained access to warm seas, allowing it to relax economically. If Afghan Mujahideen had not resisted, the USSR would not have collapsed economically.

d) Nationalists are against sectarianism.

Sectarianism is one of the sensitive issues for the Idealist movement, which is in harmony with history and looks at history objectively. For idealists who aim to develop relations among Turks, commonalities should be emphasized and strengthened. Respect should be shown for differences, and sectarian differences should be valued as diversity, not a cause for conflict. The Ottomans and Safavids became the centers of the two sects. They fought wars for three hundred years, where victory seemed impossible. The Ottoman army entered Iran, captured Tabriz, and then withdrew when winter approached. The Safavids returned and took Tabriz back. This cycle continued with neither side gaining a clear advantage. Both Turkish states weakened each other, and Russia eventually defeated both, occupying their territories. Anatolian

Turks lost their empire and could only regain Anatolia through the War of Independence. Iran also suffered losses, losing northern Azerbaijan and the Caucasus to Russia, while the Pahlavi dynasty of Persian origin came to power. However, in the following period, the occupation of northern Iran (Azerbaijan) first by Tsarist Russia and then by the Soviets, as well as the assimilationist pressure on southern Azerbaijan by the Persian nationalist Pahlavi dynasty, strengthened national consciousness. Turkey's acceptance of secularism as a principle of the republic and Azerbaijan's adoption of a secular regime upon gaining independence, despite being of the same sect, minimized the significance of sectarian differences. Moreover, during the Karabakh War, Turkey's full support for Azerbaijan and its resilience against all pressures, in contrast to Iran, which supported Armenia despite being of the same sect, reduced the sectarian difference to a minor detail. The fact that all Turkish states are secular and that the populations of all states, except Azerbaijan, are of the same sect is an advantage for the Turks. Secularism in states prevents sectarian-based divisions and highlights commonalities that encompass all societies, such as Turkishness and Islam. The problem that consumed two Turkish peoples in the past seems to have lost its effect today. Despite sectarian differences, the two peoples have become "one nation, two states."

e) Idealists are the edge.

The Idealist Movement has always been the voice of the voiceless, the advocate for those on the margins, and the breath of those left in the corners. It has represented those on the sidelines, bringing them to the center. The masses who were disconnected from the state, alienated from the government, were integrated with the state and took ownership of it thanks to the policies of the Idealist Movement. The social foundation on which the Turkish state relies was strengthened. The unity and harmony between the state and the people were achieved. The nationalist movement is, in every sense of the word, the cement of Turkey.

When Türkeş became the General Chairman of CKMP (Nationalist Movement Party), there were two Turkeys. One was the impoverished, destitute, and hungry people, and the other was the prosperous elite. 80% of the people were living on the brink of starvation. The remaining 20% consisted of the privileged, businessmen, traders, large shopkeepers, landowners, bureaucrats, and civil servants. The majority of this group also had modest means, but they were considered wealthy when compared to the general population. The happy minority, confined to areas like Ulus and Kızılay in Ankara, Harbiye, Şişli, Beyoğlu, and Nişantaşı in Istanbul, and Konak and Kordon in Izmir, had adopted a Westernized lifestyle and were distinct from the common people who lived in ignorance, poverty, and deprivation. The majority of the population had been living lives similar to their ancestors for centuries. Technology had not yet reached Anatolia.

The Republic was founded after eleven years of continuous warfare. The Tripolitanian War, the Balkan Wars, World War I, and the War of Independence followed one after the other. World War I lasted for eleven long years for the Turks while it was four years for other nations. When the Republic was established, the citizens and the nation were completely exhausted. Resources were scarce. Atatürk worked tirelessly with limited resources to develop the country and transform society through his reforms. He also established numerous industrial facilities. During the time when İnönü was the Prime Minister and Bayar was the General Manager of İş Bank (a Turkish bank), the primary engine for economic development was generally the bank. Most of the industrial facilities were either established by the bank or supported with loans. The government was occupied with implementing the reforms, expanding them, and investing in infrastructure. Education and the fight against infectious diseases were among the most important achievements of the early years. The Great Depression, which began in 1929, harmed the young Republic, which was still in the process of recovery. Borrowing from abroad or attracting foreign investment became impossible. Dissatisfied with İnönü's performance, Atatürk appointed Bayar to lead the economy. Bayar prepared the first five-year development plan and achieved its goals in less than five years. The second five-year plan was not realized due to reasons such as the death of Atatürk, İnönü's election as President, Bayar leaving the Prime Ministry, and the outbreak of World War II. The second Five-Year Plan was implemented in the early years of the Democrat Party. İnönü's years were economically challenging. While İnönü successfully managed foreign policy during the war years, he managed the economy poorly. Measures taken under the pretext of wartime often led to scarcity and deprivation. The state collected the wheat and other grains from the peasants as well as their oxen. As the state didn't have silos or storage facilities, the wheat spoiled, and the hungry oxen died. Despite having higher yields in almost all products compared to previous years, basic food items such as bread, flour, and sugar were rationed. The peasants were turned into the thieves of their own produce. Beating by the gendarmerie was a common practice. In other words, the country was in a state of collapse when the war ended. Due to the death of the oxen and the inability to find seed crops, fields couldn't be sown, and the actual yields decreased. The state, which did not have silos, had to buy flour from abroad. Thus, it became a beggar state. When the state was mentioned, people associated it with beatings, taxes, and forced labor. The 20% segment was economically better off compared to the common people. Otherwise, bureaucrats, civil servants, and shopkeepers also led modest lives. The only difference was economic. The minority fully embraced the reforms, Western culture, and values, while the majority had partial exposure to the reforms (such as primary, middle, and high schools, health centers, and the hat) and continued their traditional way of life. Right-wing governments quickly improved the economic situation of this marginalized, excluded, and forgotten segment. They did not impose a forced transformation on their way of life; instead, they respected it. As the periphery became part of the center, the center was no longer a single color but became diverse. Various groups representing every culture, belief, and way of life in the country were formed in the center. Through right-wing governments, the center grew, and the periphery diminished. As the center expanded, Turkey grew stronger. Large segments of the population integrated with the state, took ownership of it, and became loyal to the state. The Idealist Movement separated the concept of the 'state' from the concept of the 'regime,' which had been severely damaged during the single-party rule. The regime needed to change, but the state was sacred. Despite its mistakes and shortcomings, the state should be preserved because it was the embodiment of independence. All Turks who lost their state were enslaved over time. Thus, the Idealist Movement built a young and resilient segment of society ready to dedicate their lives, even to die for the state

Until the AK Party came to power, in the period leading up to it, there were certain lifestyles imposed or expected in some central areas. This imposition left behind those who did not compromise on their way of life, even if they became economically prosperous. For example, if you wore a headscarf, you couldn't work in public institutions. Before February 28, headscarves were allowed for students in universities, but they were banned after February 28. During the AK Party's rule, the headscarf issue was resolved, and the influence of religious orders and movements was expanded. This way, a significant portion of the population that had become alienated from the state took ownership of it. The sections of society that could never fully embrace the republic from its inception, which had problems with the reforms, came to the center thanks to the cooperation between the MHP (Nationalist Movement Party) and the AK Party. The Islamists, Nationalists, religious orders, and movements were molded into a state-centric nationalism, internalizing the state. These groups merged and integrated with the Idealists (Ülkücüler).

It should be emphasized that there has never been a caste system in any Turkish community. In the state system, channels for advancement were open to hardworking, ambitious, and intelligent individuals. These channels were active even in the late Ottoman period. Atatürk, İsmet Pasha, or Enver Pasha came from humble families. The state identified and educated intelligent children and turned them into leaders. Since its establishment, Turkey opened schools in every corner of the country. Boarding schools were established to provide opportunities for bright children from less privileged backgrounds to receive an education and rise in society. This method is strategic and effectively moved individuals from the periphery to the center, but its impact was limited. Right-wing governments, through their economic and social policies, brought various segments of society to the center. Despite being founded a quarter of a century after the CHP (Republican People's Party), DP (Democrat Party) was the first party to organize in the Southeastern Anatolia Region. DP aimed to reach and integrate all the marginalized, excluded, or self-excluded segments. The nationalist movement, through its widespread "Ülkü Ocakları" (Idealist Hearths) organization, reached even the most remote segments. Idealist Hearths have a presence in every corner of Turkey and are one of the most common structures, second only to mosques. Young people begin attending Idealist Hearths from an early age. Regardless of their financial means, they easily access thousands of books and computers. They participate in discussions, attend seminars, conferences, and travel across the country. Thanks to Idealist Hearths, young people first learn about, embrace, and love their nation and state. Then they develop ideals. They are guided towards higher education. Those who cannot attend courses prepare for high school or university with the help of their "ağabey" (elder brother) from the Idealist Hearth.

F) Being Pragmatic

One of the strongest aspects of the Nationalist Movement is its pragmatism, not ideology. Idealists (Ülkücüler) base their policies on the Nine Light Doctrine and adapt them to the current conditions. They have no fanaticism. The nationalist movement looks at the world through the window of Turkey and prioritizes the interests of the nation.

Türkeş was often accused of being a supporter of NATO, but he did not hesitate to clash with NATO when necessary. Türkeş signed the decision to close American bases and send American personnel abroad in response to the embargo imposed on Turkey due to the Cyprus landing. After 1990, Idealists advocated for the improvement of relations with Russia, which had been their enemy when it was communist. They supported a more independent foreign policy now that the communist threat had subsided. They emphasized the importance of establishing cooperation with Russia, as it would narrow down the maneuvering space of the United States.

The Nationalist Movement, being pragmatic, is not dogmatic, meaning it has no taboos. Hence, their scope is broad. Nationalists have principles that they refer to as doctrine. It is essential not to go against these principles. There is a significant difference between doctrine and dogma. Dogmas are defined in the finest detail, and one cannot deviate from them. Principles, on the other hand, are general, and strategies are developed based on them, taking into account the circumstances of the time.

G) Service Politics and Developmentism

In the Ottoman Empire, up until the Tanzimat period, services and investments were generally carried out through endowments (vakıflar). With the Tanzimat reforms, the Ottoman Empire transformed into a modern Western-style state. The only Ottoman Sultan who successfully implemented a service-based politics was Sultan Abdulhamid II. When he ascended to the throne, conflicts that would turn into the 1877-78 Russo-Turkish War had already begun. The Sultan made efforts to prevent war, as the army was quite weak. In fact, the Russian Tsar did not want war either. However, there were powerful lobbies and statesmen on both sides who desired war. Despite the Sultan's resistance, the Ottoman Parliament decided to go to war due to the efforts of Mithat Pasha. The

Ottoman armies were defeated in the war, and extensive territories were lost. The Sultan disbanded the parliament and consolidated power, effectively ruling the country without war for 31 years, except for the victorious Greco-Turkish War. Abdulhamid not only paid off the majority of the debts he inherited (over 90%), but also undertook massive projects.

Abdulhamid II constructed nearly all of the railways built before the republic, except for a small section of the Aydın-İzmir railway. The Berlin-Baghdad Railway and the Hejaz Railway were two immense projects of his era. Railways were critical at the time because they facilitated the transportation of goods, leading to a rapid and exponential increase in agricultural production. Producers would only produce what they needed if they were not located near production centers, ports, or railways. Excess production was meaningless because there were no means of transportation. Only highly valuable products like spices, silk, and tobacco were transported by camels as it was economical. Abdulhamid II constructed over 5,000 kilometers of railways and built hundreds of schools, irrigation canals, fountains, clock towers, textile workshops, and industrial facilities. The clock towers may seem meaningless today, but they introduced the concept of time to Ottoman people. Except for prayer times, there was no concept of time regulation for Ottomans.

After Abdulhamid, a series of wars ensued, and investments came to a halt. The construction of railways, schools, and industrial facilities restarted during Atatürk's era. Numerous projects were carried out with limited resources. During İnönü's presidency, service politics were interrupted. İnönü did not build even 100 meters of railway during his presidency. Service politics were reinitiated with Bayar and Menderes. In contrast to Abdulhamid and Atatürk, DP faced opposition during their rule. CHP never provided constructive opposition, did not point out deficiencies, and did not develop bigger and more ambitious projects. They only criticized the services and projects. When Menderes built Vatan Avenue, Edirne Road (today's E-5), Büyükdere Avenue, Millet Avenue, Barbaros Boulevard, and the Coastal Road, they opposed it, saying, "Why do you need such wide roads? Are you going to land airplanes?" DP brought up the idea of the Bosphorus Bridge and Southeastern Anatolia Project (GAP), but İnönü opposed them. He even said about the Bosphorus Bridge, "We will destroy it." While DP was working on the bridge, GAP, and other projects, CHP consistently opposed them. This shows the CHP mentality. They do not consider electricity production before consumption. They do not think about how you can consume something that has not been produced. Right-wing governments built Keban and many other dams. Ecevit, despite claiming to follow a people-centric policy, continued İnönü's approach in opposition, as seen when he opposed the Bosphorus Bridge. When AK Party lost its majority in parliament in 2018, MHP could have taken numerous ministerial positions. This would have been the natural course of events, and it was unimaginable before Bahçeli. However, MHP supported the government without taking any ministries. This sincere attitude led to a productive collaboration when AK Party responded in kind. Thanks to MHP's genuine stance, the Turkish people were introduced to the concept of constructive opposition.

H) Respectful Secularism with Freedom of Belief

MHP places importance on secularism. MHP's understanding of secularism differs from CHP's Jacobin approach. CHP used to be against any form of religious expression in public life. Headscarved individuals couldn't be civil servants, teachers, or police officers. Even university students couldn't wear headscarves. People were allowed to practice their religion at home, attend mosques, and learn about their faith, but schools couldn't provide religious education or train imams. Sufi lodges and religious sects were not tolerated. However, with the transition to a multi-party system, CHP's Jacobin approach softened. Religious vocational courses, which would later evolve into Imam Hatip schools, were established. Elective religious courses were introduced in schools. CHP didn't oppose the reversion of the call to prayer to its original form in the mosques. MHP supports religious education in schools. It believes that citizens should be educated in their faith, and the state should cultivate religious clergy with a sense of Turkish identity. As long as religious groups don't engage in terrorist activities, oppose the state, or violate the law, they should be free to operate. People can believe in whatever they want, defend their beliefs, and live their lives accordingly. The state shouldn't interfere in people's private lives unless they harm others.

As the population became more religious, conservative leaders also embraced religious values. The concept of secularism went through a transformation. Bayar, despite being a devout and knowledgeable Muslim, didn't attend the mosque while he was President because of his commitment to secularism. He would wait for foreign heads of state during their prayers. However, Menderes, who was religious, used to participate in prayers and religious events, both with foreign heads of state and on special occasions or religious nights. Although he didn't go to the mosque regularly, he sometimes attended Friday prayers. Demirel didn't miss Friday prayers, he would wear a prayer cap and would always perform his prayers. His act of going to Friday prayers in his official car in 1965 was considered revolutionary. It was known that Menderes had met with respected religious scholars like Said Nursi and Süleyman Efendi and supported publications with a religious theme, such as Büyük Doğu. Demirel, who inherited these relationships from Menderes, developed them further. He welcomed members of religious orders into the party, attended events organized by religious sects and orders, and organized iftar dinners attended by thousands of citizens during Ramadan. He appointed individuals who represented these religious groups as members of parliament. Demirel had received religious education from Hafız Ali, a student of Said Nursi, and was highly knowledgeable about Risale-i Nur. Demirel used to base his speeches on important messages from the Quran and Hadith. Özal had affiliations with religious orders and was a follower of Mehmet Zahit Kotku. When he became Undersecretary of the State Planning Organization (DPT) in 1966, he opened a mosque within the organization. His reputation included going around in wooden sandals for ablutions and wearing a prayer cap. He also had a mosque built when he became the Prime Minister. These practices were considered the natural outcome of secularism, but during the early years of the republic, the authoritarian understanding of secularism prevailed. As a result, these practices were interpreted as being against secularism rather than being in line with it. Türkeş used to pray the Friday prayers with a congregation. He was one of the first leaders of the Turkish nation who had a strong sense of religious identity. After returning from the Hajj, the titles "Hacı" and "Hacı Albay" were added to his name in military and political gatherings. Türkeş visited religious scholars more extensively than any other leader, including some practices that other leaders did not engage in. During party congresses, he would have religious scholars sit next to him. The four right-wing leaders were not concerned with the religious affiliations of their political colleagues or bureaucrats.

İ) MHP is unifying.

Central Asia, from the 15th century onwards, received the migration of Kipchak groups known as Uzbeks in three waves, attributed to the Golden Horde Khan and named after Uzbek Khan. The Uzbeks who arrived in three waves merged with the settled Karluks in the region, forming the Uzbek society. By transitioning to a settled way of life, Uzbeks who settled in the west of Turkistan and those who settled in the east became known as "Karluks," with their spoken dialect initially called Uighur and later Chagatai. To the north of the Karluks, covering a vast geographical area extending from China to Central Europe, lived the Turks, and their spoken dialect was referred to as Kipchak Turkish. In the west of the Karluks and to the south of the Kipchaks lived the Turks, and their spoken dialect was Oghuz Turkish. Kazakhs, Kyrgyz, Karakalpaks, Tatars, Bashkirs, Chuvash, Avars, and Yakut Turks speak the Kipchak dialect, and their languages are quite similar, enabling easy mutual understanding. Turks from Turkmenistan, Azerbaijan, Turkey, Iran, and Gagauzia are Oghuz Turks. Their spoken dialects are highly similar to each other. Uzbeks and Uighurs speak the sub-dialects of Chagatai Turkish.

Karluks founded empires such as the Karakhanid, Ghaznavid, Chagatai, Uighur, Timurid, and Mughal. Kipchaks established dominions alongside the Volga, in the regions of the Idil Bulgar, Hazar, Mamluk, Golden Horde, and after the fall of the Golden Horde, they founded khanates like Crimea, Kazan, Astrakhan, Nogai, Siberia, and Kasim Khanates, along with the Kazakh and Uzbek Khanates. The Oghuz Turks, on the other hand, were responsible for the establishment of empires such as the Seljuk, Khwarezm-Shah, Aq Qoyunlu, Qara Qoyunlu, Safavid, and Ottoman.

The Idealists consider their belonging to the Turkish nation as their primary identity. They do not distinguish between Oghuz, Karluks, and Kipchaks, or the peoples that constitute these three groups. Before the invasion of Tsarist Russia, being a Turkistanli in Central Asia was a common identity. First the Russian Empire and then the USSR blurred the definitions of Turkistan, Turk, and Turkistanli, emphasizing Uzbek, Kazakh, Kyrgyz, Tatar, Turkmen, Tajik, and Bashkir identities instead. They even attempted to foster animosity among the Turkic peoples. The Idealist movement aims for the unity of all Turkic peoples under the Turkish umbrella while also respecting sub-identities like the Kazakhs, Kyrgyz, Turkmen, Yakuts, and Gagauz. A similar approach applies to local relationships based on hometown or place of origin. Almost all parts of the Turkic world are afflicted by hometown relationships. A significant portion of citizens prioritizes loyalty to hometown over merit and intellect. Being from the same hometown is an unwritten rule for employment in the public sector. Hometown relationships are prevalent in almost every field and play a determining role. The Idealists value the love, respect, and mutual assistance among hometown residents. However, they are against hometown relationships that go beyond this framework and almost replace national loyalty. Their most important identity is being a member of the Turkish nation. They value sub-identities that don't undermine this membership.

J) Nationalism

The MHP's philosophy of nationalism is inclusive, not divisive. Their concept of the nation is not based on race but on culture. This ideology is encapsulated by Atatürk's statement, "How happy is the one who says, 'I am a Turk!'" He did not say, "How happy is the one who is born a Turk" or "How happy is the one who becomes a Turk." Demirel's definition, "From the Adriatic to the Great Wall of China, the Turkish World," aptly conveys the MHP's perspective. He did not say, "From Edirne to the Great Wall of China" because he also considered Turkish communities in Western Thrace and Bulgaria, taking the Karasu River to the Great Wall of China into account. The term "Adriatic" includes Albanians, Bosniaks, and Kosovars. The reference to the Great Wall of China encompasses the Caucasus and even the Circassians. In other words, the Turkish nation is not defined by its ethnic origins. The Turkish nation is a inclusive community created by people, regardless of their ethnic background, who speak Turkish, adhere to Turkish-Islamic culture, share a common history, aspire to a common future, and have a will to live together. According to the MHP, the most significant identity is belonging to the nation. From a Turkish perspective, it means being a citizen. Hometown, ethnic affiliation, tribe, religious or sectarian belonging are all valuable and respected, but citizenship is the primary identity. The bond of citizenship should be strengthened.

The MHP, as a consequence of its nationalism principle, is republican and supports the unitary state. It opposes structures like federations or autonomous regions. Upholding the people's will, embracing the nation's values, and exalting the nation are the requirements of nationalism. Demirel's definition of "From the Adriatic to the Great Wall of China" did not suddenly emerge in 1991. It is the definition of the policy implemented by center-right governments since 1950. The center-right acknowledged the migrations from this region. Menderes, accepting those who suffered oppression in the Balkans, Central Asia, and East Turkestan, welcomed them, granted them citizenship, and allocated land. This approach was continued by all center-right governments. However, the CHP's approach was different. İnönü did not accept immigrants from these regions and even returned those who sought refuge, knowing they would face execution in their home countries. During World War II, the extradition of Azerbaijani Turks who took refuge in our lands is an example of the CHP's policies. In 195, those being returned were executed on the Boraltan Bridge, where the extradition took place. What sets the MHP apart from other right-wing parties is their consistent focus on the issue of "Captive Turks." They work on matters related to Turks living abroad and make efforts to establish connections. The collapse of the USSR and the independence of Turkic states validate the MHP's foresight. The MHP is not only interested in external Turks but also in the Turkish expatriates working in Western countries. The Turkish Federation, first established in Europe and later in America and Australia, has become the second home for Turkish expatriates. The federation makes efforts for the new generations born abroad to grow up as Muslim Turks.

k) Spirituality

MHP is committed to spiritual values. Spiritual values are the main element that constitutes the nation. Preserving, enhancing, and passing on these spiritual values to future generations is the fundamental goal. A society that weakens its spiritual values, even if it is wealthy, loses the essence of being a nation. The will to live together gradually diminishes. The most significant spiritual value of the Turkish nation is Islam. The overwhelming majority of citizens are Muslims. Islam serves as the adhesive that binds society both to each other and to the past and the future. Therefore, the understanding of secularism among Idealists (MHP supporters) is not as strict as that of the CHP (Republican People's Party). MHP has provided unconditional support for introducing religious education in schools, establishing religious vocational schools (imam-hatip), Quran courses, and theology faculties. The activities of religious communities and orders that do not conflict with the state were both supported and monitored. MHP opposes the Salafi-Wahhabi ideology that rejects the accumulated tradition of Islam spanning more than 1400 years. They consider political Islam that alienates young people from their own society and ideologies that are antagonistic to the nation and nationalism to be dangerous.

L) Being in Favor of the Welfare State

The MHP is in favor of a free-market economy but does not endorse the American-style capitalism philosophy of "let the fallen fall, and what remains is ours." Their approach is to aim at reaching the needy segments of society. Türkeş, through his Nine Lights (Dokuz Işık) framework, emphasized the importance of distributing income to the grassroots. Their goal is to elevate the welfare level of the lower and middle-income groups. In Turkish culture, the ruler, which is the state or hakan, has always been responsible for "feeding the hungry and clothing the naked." The MHP's understanding of the welfare state is rooted in this principle. Türkeş advocated for the establishment of a versatile "Social Solidarity Board" from the early days of his political career.

M) Being at Peace with History

MHP is objective in its approach to history, as it does not view history through an ideological lens. It is not biased. It respects the Ottoman Empire but is not Ottomanist. It demonstrates its respect for the Ottoman Empire by incorporating the three crescents into the party emblem. MHP holds great respect for Mustafa Kemal Atatürk as a heroic statesman who led the War of Independence and established the republic, but it is not Kemalist.

MHP does not give in to dogmas. It respects Atatürk but does not believe he was infallible. MHP respects anyone who has served the country but evaluates them objectively. For example, for Kemalists, Sultan Abdulhamid II is the "Red Sultan." For adherents of National Vision, he is the "Great Sultan." For nationalists, he is one of the successful sultans who served the country. However, there is no doubt that he had his share of mistakes and shortcomings.

MHP is not polarizing but unifying and integrating. It does not take sides between individuals who confronted each other in history, it does not pit them against each other. Atatürk is the founder of the republic, Mehmet Akif is a great patriot, and Abdülhakim Arvasi is an important intellectual who served religion. Being at peace with history allows for an objective perspective. When one is objective, historical events are evaluated correctly, and lessons are learned.

Idealists (Ülkücüler) view Turkish history as a whole. They objectively evaluate every period of Turkish history. Islamists, by dismissing the pre-Islamic history of the Turks, lose the ability to evaluate and interpret Turkish history properly. Kemalists, by ignoring the Ottoman Empire and denigrating all aspects of that era, commit a similar error from a different angle. Far-left movements that interpret history as a class struggle and see everything as a derivative of this struggle are already highly subjective.

Idealists (Ülkücüler) accept Turkish history as a whole and focus on the nation. They do not see history only as a source of pride. They do not shy away from confronting mistakes, errors, and shortcomings. Among the Turkish people, nationalists have the highest historical awareness and consciousness in the Turkish world.

N) To be against any kind of coup.

MHP is against any kind of coup, no matter who the perpetrators may be, and it does not accept guardianship. Türkeş, having been involved in the May 27 coup, realized through experience how dangerous coups, coup attempts, and junta actions could be. Türkeş's statement, "The worst democratic rule is far better than the best dictatorship," is the product of these experiences. Some political commentators portray İnönü as a democracy hero because he opposed coup attempts due to his position as Prime Minister. İnönü opposed coup attempts because he was the Prime Minister. If these attempts had been successful, he would have lost his premiership. He was protecting his own power, not democracy. On the other hand, Aydemir was against democracy and what he called the party regime; had he been successful, he would have established a dictatorship. If İnönü were truly a democrat, he would have opposed the May 27 and

March 12 coups when he was in the opposition. However, Türkeş turned down the offer to become one of the leaders of the coup when it was proposed to him. He warned Aydemir and Gürcan. When he received information that coup preparations were ongoing, he ensured that this information reached the authorities. Türkeş was always against the military's involvement in politics.

The growth rates achieved by right-wing parties when they came to power alone in the same years are not lower than the rates achieved by Germany, Korea, and Japan. However, Germany and Japan did not face coups. In Korea, the coup plotters were well-versed in economics and strategically managed not to lower the growth rates. In Turkey, on the other hand, coups and the transition periods following coups resulted in very low growth rates, and sometimes even economic contraction, causing the country to fall behind rival nations. If Turkey had experienced seventy years without coups, like Japan and Germany, it would be at a similar economic level with them today.

O) MHP is a leader-centric and organizational party.

MHP has widespread and strong organizations. In right-wing parties, the most important figure is the leader. Success is brought about by the connection the leader establishes with the party members and the masses. If the leader cannot capture the same spirit and frequency as the masses, no matter what the organization does, success cannot be achieved. Especially in the MHP, the leader is more important than in any other party. The leader is called the Başbuğ. Başbuğ is the leader of the Turks. Just as Mete in the Huns, Atilla in the European Huns, Bilge Han in the Göktürks, Alparslan in the Seljuks, and Fatih in the Ottomans were, Türkeş is the leader of the Turks. MHP organizations are predominantly young and, therefore, energetic. Idealists believe that they are the army of Allah. They work and engage in activities with the excitement of serving the great Turkish nation and Turan.

MHP appeals to all segments of society. It accommodates people with different views and beliefs within its ranks. Nationalism is the common denominator. They are respectful of religion. They support the freedom for citizens to practice their beliefs as they wish, but they have no intention of structuring the state according to the rules of religion. MHP aims to develop the country, enrich the citizens, and distribute income to the base. They are committed to national and spiritual values because these values are what make the nation a nation.

P) MHP is Republican and Democratic.

MHP is republican. It is against monarchy. Türkeş and Bahçeli, as well as the core of society, belong to the periphery, the rural areas. They attained their positions thanks to the republic and democracy. They did not equate religion with the republic, nor did they compare Turkey with the Ottoman Empire. The nation's religion is Islam, and the country's governing system is a democratic republic. Turkey is the continuation of the Ottoman Empire. The Ottoman Empire was the most magnificent state founded by the Turkish nation, but it was history. The people greatly favored the democratic republic. They participated in elections in high numbers, filled rally squares whenever they had the opportunity, and did not welcome coups. In most European countries that were historically ruled by monarchies, there are still monarchist parties. In Turkey, since the transition to democracy, hundreds of parties have been established, but not a single monarchist party has emerged. This is because the people had no inclination toward monarchy. Even within democracy, the people did not allow the establishment of dynasties. The sons of Adnan Menderes, who was deeply loved, could only become deputies. Aydın Menderes, despite forming a party, could not secure popular support. The same situation applies to Turgut Özal's brothers, Yusuf and Korkut Özal, and his son Ahmet Özal. The fact that Bayar's son-in-law was an outstanding politician. If he hadn't married Bayar's daughter, he could have risen to better positions. Nilüfer Gürsoy, Bayar's daughter, had a long political career but was never considered for leadership. Besides, Bayar had an adult son. Turgut Bayar was never considered for the leadership of the AP. The party founded by Türkeş's son never made any impact. The DYP delegate did not support Kesici, Demirel's son-in-law, and did not embrace him. The overwhelming majority of the public is against all forms of dynastic rule.

Q) Idealists aim to increase public support for the state.

The loyalty of Turkic communities to their states is the strength of Turkish states. In an international survey conducted by a reputable organization, Turks emerged as the people most loyal to their states.

When asked, "Would you be willing to fight for your country and, if necessary, sacrifice your life?" Azerbaijani Turks responded with 85%, Turkish Turks with 73%, and Kazakh Turks with 69%, answering, "I would sacrifice my life." Taking into consideration that around 25% of Kazakhstan's population has Slavic roots, it can be understood that the rate is even higher among the Kazakh-origin citizens. Similar statistics in Germany are at 18%, the Netherlands at 15%, and Spain at 21%. Since the survey didn't cover all Turkish regions, we don't have data for the others, but it can be assumed that similar rates would appear. Every state should aim to have its society fully embrace and support it. No amount of state pressures, support, or incentives can change the situation if the society the state relies on has become alienated from the state. States should emphasize the commonalities that constitute society and build on those as much as possible. Respect should be shown for the differences within society, and a wide environment of freedom should be provided for different beliefs, faiths, and lifestyles. For instance, the majority of Turkish society is Muslim. While the vast majority of Muslim Turks are Sunni, there are also Alevi, Shiite, and Nusayri groups, along with Christian and Jewish communities in Turkey. The Turkish state should prioritize Islamic values that all Muslims can accept, while providing an environment in which Christians and Jews can freely and openly practice their beliefs. If the Islamic values emphasized are only appealing to Sunnis, non-Sunnis will feel excluded. The state's support base will narrow, and it won't reach many of its citizens. Therefore, the state should be a gathering point for as many different beliefs, faiths, ways of life, and cultures as possible. An important aim for leaders is to ensure this. In the U.S., the descendants of people who were enslaved for centuries proudly say, "I'm American." The statistics from the survey are quite high, but looking at the reverse side of the coin, 27% of Turkish citizens, and 31% of Kazakh citizens have clearly and firmly said that they would not fight and die for their homeland. Turkish states should aim to reduce these high negative figures by conducting research to understand why they are so high. Like individuals, communities can have multiple identities, affiliations, and identities that make up their identity. As a society develops and its civilization level rises, the number of affiliations increases. It is not necessary for every member of society to embrace and care about these affiliations; it is enough if the vast majority of society does. An ordinary citizen might describe themselves as a "Muslim, Turkish person." In addition to this, religious sect, place of origin, residence, sports team support, and gender are the primary affiliations that shape an individual's identity. For some individuals, a religious sect, Sufi order, or their favorite sports team may be their primary affiliation. The same situation holds true within societies. Societies are not homogenous masses, but rather they are composed of individuals with various identities, affiliations, and beliefs. When one says "Greek Nation," we typically think of a Christian, Orthodox, Mediterranean, and European society. In reality, many Greeks are atheists or have no connection to Orthodoxy. Yet, Christianity and Orthodoxy are the dominant elements in Greek national identity. The more inclusive a state identity is, the more citizens will internalize and identify with it.

R) Idealists (Ülkücüler) are against population planning.

Türkeş, when he entered politics, has been consistently against family planning. Devlet Bahçeli continued along the same line. Since 1965, Türkeş has constantly mentioned a Turkey with a population of 100 million. He emphasized that the Anatolian lands could easily sustain a population of 100 million. Türkeş supported and encouraged industrialists but always kept his distance from Vehbi Koç. The primary reason for this was Vehbi Koç's strong support for family planning. Turkish nationalists consider the population to be one of the main elements that make a nation strong. Turkish population is regularly increasing at reasonable rates. Looking at current trends, when population growth stops, the population remains stable for a short time and then rapidly declines. Population decrease means aging and a decrease in productivity. Once the population starts to decrease, it's very difficult, if not impossible, to reverse the trend. The most critical ratio to consider when evaluating the population is the fertility rate per woman or per family. The fertility rate should be slightly above 2 per family. This is necessary to maintain the population because not everyone gets married, and some couples remain childless or have only one child. Thus, a fertility rate of 2.2 to 2.5 per family is considered ideal for renewing the population and ensuring continued productivity. In less wealthy countries, population growth rates exceeding 2.5 can lead to unemployment and poverty, creating problems. When we approach the issue from the perspective of states, it becomes more explanatory. The population of a society on which a state relies is its human power. Human power is the most important power for states because all other powers are derivatives of human power. Factors such as the population of the society, education level, economic status, dynamism, average age, and loyalty to the state make up human power. The state is responsible for improving all the factors that constitute human power. Serious deterioration in factors that constitute human power can threaten the existence of both the nation and the state in the medium and long term, regardless of how strong the state is. For example, in Russia and Japan, the population is decreasing. In Russia, in addition to the decrease in the number of ethnic Russians, the number of Turkic peoples is increasing. No matter how good the economy is or how high the rate of development, these cannot solve the problem of population decrease. This problem means that in a century, Russia will no longer be Russia. It means a constantly aging and decreasing population, just like Japan.   Türk Ülkeleri Doğurganlık Oranları

Tabii ki, işte Türk ülkelerinin doğurganlık oranlarının İngilizce çevirisi:

Turkic Countries Fertility Rates

Year 2000 | Year 2020

- Turkmenistan | 3.63 | 2.70
- Tajikistan | 4.35 | 3.24
- Kyrgyzstan | 3.22 | 3.00
- Turkey | 3.20 | 1.92
- Uzbekistan | 3.09 | 2.90
- Azerbaijan | 2.19 | 1.70
- Kazakhstan | 2.03 | 3.13

As can be seen from the table, fertility rates in the Turkic states outside Kazakhstan are decreasing. It is quite normal for fertility to decline in urbanized and highly educated societies. The critical point is that the rate does not drop below 2.50. If you pay attention, you'll see that Azerbaijan's rate is both very low and consistently decreasing. Without taking necessary measures at this stage, Azerbaijan will join the list of countries with a declining and aging population. Turkey's situation is even more dramatic. In 2021 (1.71), the declining trend continued, and the rate of decrease even accelerated. From a state's perspective, the rapid decline of fertility rates over a very short period of fewer than twenty years should set off alarm bells for Turkey. If the decline continues, Turkey will lose all its dynamism. In Kazakhstan, the increase in the fertility rate in 2000 can be attributed to significant Russian migration in the 1990s and early 2000s. In 2000, the birth rate among Kazakh women was high. The low birth rate among Russians was pulling the average rate down. Another reason for the high rate among Kazakhs is the rapid economic development of Kazakhstan. The current situation proves that opposing family planning is the right course of action. Without precautions, population growth is about to stop in Turkey and Azerbaijan. Then, the population will remain stable for a short time, followed by a decline. Aging of the population will follow. Germany's fertility rate in 2019 was 1.54. This rate means that the population is halved in two generations and continues to age each year. Germany addresses the labor shortage by importing three hundred thousand foreign workers each year. However, no matter how selective they are, the balance of the population is disturbed. Moreover, the 1.54 rate is an average for Germany. The fertility rate of ethnic Germans in Germany is even lower. Russia's fertility rate in 2019 was 1.50. This rate was 1.25 in 2000 and 1.40 in 2008. After Putin became president, Russia increased population growth by supporting and encouraging it. Despite these policies, Russia's demographic problem cannot be solved. While the birth rate of Russians is very low, the birth rate of Russian citizens of Turkic descent is quite high. After the collapse of the Soviet Union, Russia received significant Russian migration from Eastern Europe, the Baltic States, the Balkans, and former Soviet Union countries. Russia has granted citizenship to Russians and even Slavs residing outside Russia. Russia also annexed Crimea. Despite all this, in 31 years, the population did not increase; it decreased. During the same period, Turkey's population increased from 52 million to 85 million. Additionally, Russia's Russian population rate decreased from over 80% to less than 70%. While Russians in the East and rural areas are migrating to Western Russia, including cities like Moscow and St. Petersburg, where ethnic Russians are the majority. Throughout the Autonomous Turkic Republics, where Turks are a minority, Turks have become the majority. In Russia-China border areas, while Russians are decreasing, the Chinese population is rapidly increasing. To sustain its production level, Russia accepts three hundred thousand foreign workers every year. The majority of these foreign workers are Uzbeks, Kyrgyz, and Tajiks. Over time, most of these workers become citizens. In the long run, the population of Turks is increasing because of those who later become citizens. Independent Turkic states, especially Turkey and Azerbaijan, need to create policies and strategies regarding population growth; otherwise, the strong aspect of the Turkish nation's population will become weaker. The population of Turks who are citizens of other countries is increasing steadily. Especially in Russia and Iran, the demographic balance is shifting in favor of Turks. The population of Turks has decreased in regions due to migration. These regions include Afghanistan, Syria, and Iraq. Many Turks have migrated from these three countries due to internal conflicts.

D -) THE FOREIGN POLICY CONCEPT OF THE NATIONALIST MOVEMENT

In this section, we discussed Türkeş's views and policy recommendations on key topics of Turkish foreign policy. These views have formed the basis of the Nationalist Movement's approach to foreign policy over time. Since the 1950s, Cyprus has been a central issue in Turkish foreign policy. Atatürk stated, "Gentlemen, as long as Cyprus remains in the hands of the enemy, our supply routes are blocked. Pay attention to Cyprus. This island is of great importance to us." In line with Atatürk's statement, Türkeş, during his tenure as the Prime Ministry Undersecretary, emphasized that Greece was attempting to encircle Turkey from the Çanakkale Straits to the east of Antalya using the islands. He brought up the Greek claims regarding Cyprus, which has historically never belonged to Greece, and highlighted their significance in relation to the strategic importance of the Eastern Mediterranean. Türkeş asserted that Greece was trying to block Turkey's southern exit from its ports in İskenderun, Antalya, and Mersin. He believed that the Cyprus issue should be considered a non-partisan matter, and emphasized the need for supporting it with scientific studies and defending it through diplomatic activity on the international stage.

Due to the islands in the Aegean Sea being given to Greece along the western and southwestern line, Turkey found itself almost entirely surrounded. For Turkey, Cyprus remained as the only outlet to the Mediterranean. Therefore, Türkeş considered Cyprus as not just an issue concerning the Turks living there but as a matter of national security. He argued that Cyprus was a natural extension of Turkey geologically and geographically. Thus, Türkeş insisted that Turkey should assert the principle that a country's natural extensions should belong to that country, using examples such as Kashmir, Western Thrace, South Tyrol, and Karolos Berzahi. This view is also supported by geologists since Cyprus is located only 70 kilometers away from Turkey. The 1958 Geneva Convention defines the continental shelf as extending from the point where the territorial waters end. According to this definition, any state with a coastline has rights to the continental shelf. Therefore, Türkeş believed that Cyprus should be considered a natural extension of Turkey and an inseparable part.

Additionally, Türkeş raised concerns about Greece's expansionist policies related to Cyprus, which was located 1,100 kilometers away from Greece. He emphasized that the claims of Greece regarding Cyprus were based on imperialist ambitions. Türkeş pointed out that Cyprus was a national cause, directly related to Turkey's security and defense. He continuously emphasized Greece's continuous expansion against Turkey and the fact that Greece and the Cyprus Greek administration aimed for Enosis. He criticized the oppressive treatment of Turkish Cypriots and highlighted that Greece's Megali Idea was still being kept alive.

In response to the coup by Greek officers in Cyprus on July 15, 1974, Türkeş made a statement on July 17, 1974, in which he claimed that the coup in Cyprus had achieved Enosis, the constitutional order established by the London and Zurich Agreements had been abolished, the Hellenic Republic had been established, and a new constitution had been prepared. He also claimed that the United States had consented to this situation, and he called on the Ecevit government to intervene. On July 20, 1974, the Cyprus Peace Operation began. On the same day, Türkeş issued another statement congratulating the President, the Republican government, the Chief of the General Staff, and the commanders and suggested that cooperation with allies should be established. Türkeş strongly believed that the island must be given to Turkey because it was historically a part of Turkey, it was directly related to Turkey's security, and 40% of the island's ownership belonged to Turks. Türkeş noted that the political objectives of the operation were as follows: to restore the constitutional order established by the London and Zurich Agreements, to ensure the security of Turkish Cypriots, to establish peace in Cyprus, to restore the balance achieved in the Eastern Mediterranean through the Treaty of Lausanne, and to block the path to Enosis. However, Türkeş claimed that the operation did not meet these political objectives and that it only managed to control a triangular area up to thirty kilometers deep, and the political objectives were not achieved.

Türkeş criticized the mistakes made by the Ecevit government. He pointed out that the military operation should have started immediately after the coup in Cyprus, rather than waiting for six days, which allowed for international reactions. Türkeş argued that an operation on the same day as the coup, before international reactions could mount, could have resolved the issue without problems. He also claimed that the whole island could have been taken under control in two or three days. Türkeş believed that a third operation was essential to achieve the final goal, which was taking the entire island under Turkish sovereignty. Türkeş argued that Cyprus had been effectively Turkish territory for 308 years and legally for nearly 400 years, and Greece had never had any control. Therefore, he proposed that instead of asking why Turkey won, people should ask why Greece controlled two-thirds of the island.

Furthermore, one of the main foreign policy issues for Turkey is Western Thrace. Türkeş argued that Western Thrace is not an issue that can only be assessed within the context of Turkish expatriates. He explained how Western Thrace had been left to Greece as a result of competition among global powers. He highlighted how the Treaty of Ayestefanos had made Western Thrace part of Bulgaria. However, the Berlin Agreement ensured that Western

One of Turkey's important international issues is the "Island Issue," which revolves around three main categories: the Aegean Islands, the 12 Islands, and undefined islands and islets.

The Aegean Islands were occupied by Greece during the Balkan Wars. According to the Treaty of London, the fate of the Aegean Islands was left to the Great Powers. With the Treaty of Athens, the Ottoman Empire accepted that Crete belonged to Greece. On February 13, 1914, the Great Powers informed Greece and the Ottoman Empire that the Aegean Islands were being handed over to Greece. In this note, it was stated that all the Aegean Islands, except Meis, Gökçeada, Bozcaada, and the 12 Islands, were being given to Greece. The Treaty of Lausanne, in

Article 12, recognized that, apart from Imroz, Bozcaada, and the Rabbit Islands, the other islands belonged to Greece. It was mentioned that islands within 3 miles of the Asian coast were under Turkish sovereignty. Article 13 specified that no military bases could be established on the islands handed over to Greece, and aside from internal security units, no military personnel could be stationed there.

During the Italo-Turkish War, Italy occupied the 12 Islands. According to the 1912 Treaty of Ouchy, Italy would return the 12 Islands to the Ottoman Empire. However, to prevent Greece from occupying them during the Balkan Wars, Italy held them temporarily. In the Treaty of Lausanne, Article 15 indicated that the 12 Islands and Meis were given to Italy. After Italy's defeat in World War II, the 12 Islands were first occupied by Germany and then came under British control. The Allies handed over the 12 Islands to Greece with the 1947 Paris Peace Treaties. When Greece began to militarize and establish military bases on these islands, Alparslan Türkeş evaluated the Island Issue as a matter of national security and emphasized the need for the implementation of international treaties. He pointed out that Greece was arming the islands in violation of international agreements while also occupying undefined islands. Türkeş underlined that the surrender of the islands to Greece had cut off Turkey's maritime connections and had been a national security issue for Turkey for a century.

Another significant issue for Turkey is its continental shelf. Türkeş argued that the geological maps of the seafloor of the Aegean Sea showed a rift splitting the Aegean Sea from the mouth of the Meriç River to the island of Crete, suggesting that the eastern part belonged to Turkey, and the western part to Greece. Türkeş believed that Greece's demand for a 12-mile territorial waters limit would effectively imprison Turkey in the Aegean Sea. Türkeş stressed that the Aegean Islands were among Turkey's close national goals, and he urged all Turks not to forget this national goal.

One of the most challenging issues during Turkey's founding was the Mosul Question. It could not be resolved during the Treaty of Lausanne negotiations and was postponed. The discussions, which began in 1924, did not yield results, so the matter was taken to the League of Nations. The League ruled that Mosul and its surrounding areas were part of Iraq. However, Turkey insisted on a popular referendum and only accepted that Mosul belonged to Iraq in 1926 due to Kurdish uprisings. In 1932, the

Turkey-Iraq Residence Agreement regulated the residence, work, and property ownership of Turkish citizens in Iraq, providing opportunities for Iraq's Turkmen community to come to Turkey. During the 1991 Gulf Crisis, President Özal mentioned Turkey's right to intervene in Mosul and Kirkuk, which were within the National Pact borders. Türkeş also urged Turkey to seize the opportunity to take control of Mosul and Kirkuk for national interests. Atatürk had previously offered the United States that Mosul and Kirkuk belong to Turkey in exchange for granting the U.S. oil operating rights.

During Süleyman Demirel's time as Deputy Prime Minister, he sought opportunities for cooperation with the USSR. After mutual visits, an agreement was signed in 1967 for the establishment of heavy industry facilities. Numerous heavy industrial plants were built under this agreement. When the Justice Party (AP) came to power, relations with the United States were strained, partly due to President Johnson's harshly worded letter to Prime Minister İnönü. However, these tensions escalated further after the agreement with the USSR. During Demirel's leadership, Turkey signed two strategic agreements with the United States, one of which limited the rights and powers of American personnel in Turkey. After this agreement, the United States reduced the number of its personnel in Turkey from 30,000 to 7,000. In July 1969, a Joint Defense and Cooperation Agreement was signed between the two allies, placing heavy conditions on the U.S. for establishing bases. All constructed buildings and facilities belonged to Turkey. Additionally, the U.S. couldn't remove equipment, weapons, ammunition, and other assets from Turkey without the Turkish government's permission. This clause prevented a recurrence of the Jupiter missile crisis that had occurred during the İnönü-Kennedy era. During this time, despite pressures related to the reduction of opium cultivation areas, opium cultivation continued. Türkeş, who was in opposition during these years, supported the AP government's establishment of heavy industry with the USSR, the agreements with the U.S., and the continuation of opium cultivation.

The AP changed Turkey's foreign policy approach in the Middle East compared to the Democratic Party (DP), which had followed a different path in NATO. It witnessed the coups in Egypt, Iraq, and Syria, which led to the formation of the United Arab Republic under Nasser's leadership. AP interpreted these developments as an encirclement from the south and the transformation of friendly regimes into hostile ones, so it took a different stance against coup leaders. However, during AP's term, the United Arab Republic had already dissolved, and the initial fervor and excitement of the revolutions had faded. In May 1967, just before the Arab-Israeli war, the Ministry of Foreign Affairs held a conference attended by ambassadors to determine the long-term foreign policy principles concerning Arab states. The main principles set during this conference were: 1) Strengthen relations with all Arab countries in every area, 2) Remain neutral in Arab disputes, and 3) Avoid participation in regional agreements and pacts that may divide Arabs. Following the outbreak of the Arab-Israeli war in June, when the U.S. took a pro-Israel stance, it was declared that Turkish military bases would not be used against Arab countries. Turkey provided food and clothing aid to Egypt, Jordan, and Syria and voted in favor of Arab resolutions at the United Nations. The AP government was the first to take a stance supporting the Arabs in the Palestine issue. During the 1967 war, two leaders, Türkeş, the Chairman of the Nationalist Movement Party (MHP), and Bölükbaşı, the Chairman of the Nation Party (MP), openly supported the Arabs and condemned Israel. However, İnönü, as usual, remained silent. After the war, Arab states decided to establish the Organization of the Islamic Conference (OIC) and invited Turkey to its first meeting. President Sunay declined the invitation, stating, "Turkey is a secular country and cannot participate in an ganization or a group that includes the word 'Islam.' Demirel, on the other hand, expressed his support for "Muslim states." Turkey eventually became an observer member of the OIC. Turkey continued to support Arab resolutions at the United Nations, even after the 1967 war. The main reason for the March 12 Memorandum was to stop opium cultivation, and another reason was the change in Turkey's foreign policy stance.

After the memorandum, the first action of the government led by Nihat Erim was to halt opium cultivation. They reduced relations with Arab states to their previous level. During Süleyman Demirel's time in power, he took several measures to strengthen relations with the Arab world.

Demirel, on March 31, 1975, formed the First Nationalist Front Government with CGP, MSP, and MHP. This marked the first time that the MHP was a coalition partner in power. Up until that time, during the years in opposition, Türkeş largely supported the main aspects of the foreign policy pursued by AP and the CHP-MSP government. Issues related to external Turks were brought up on every occasion. During this period, the MHP established relations with all external Turks. The majority of external Turks were living in dictatorially ruled countries such as the USSR, China, Iran, Iraq, Syria, Bulgaria, Romania, and Albania. They were subjected to great hardship, as these regimes either ignored or tried to assimilate the Turks, aiming to eradicate their identity. In Yugoslavia, where "smiling communism" was practiced, the Turkish minority had a relatively more comfortable situation. In Greece, especially during the junta period, the oppression of the Turks reached its peak. Greek governments made the Turkish minority suffer for developments in Cyprus. Relations were more easily established, especially in democratic Western countries. In the 1970s, associations following the MHP's line were founded in European countries. This was followed by the United States, Canada, and Australia. In the second half of the 1970s, associations in Europe formed country federations. These federations integrated under a confederation that addressed all of Europe.

During the CHP-MSP government's time, military intervention took place in Cyprus. Ecevit, under the influence of the intervention, resigned with the intention of forcing early elections to come to power alone. When other parties did not support early elections, Sadi Irmak's government, a non-partisan government, was formed. Despite not obtaining a vote of confidence, the Irmak government remained in power until March 31. During Irmak's government, the United States Senate decided to impose a complete embargo on Turkey by cutting off aid. Irmak strongly opposed the embargo, even though President Ford was also against it. First, Turkey sent a note to the United States, and then it declared the Turkish Federated State of Cyprus. The declaration of independence was met with strong reactions from the United States, the European Economic Community (EEC), Greece, and the Greek Cypriot administration. Despite all efforts, the Ford administration and Secretary of State Kissinger could not persuade the Senate to lift or ease the embargo. In response, Germany started providing military aid to Turkey. After forming the government, Demirel immediately initiated efforts to lift the embargo. Despite intensive diplomacy led by Çağlayangil, no progress was made. Therefore, the Demirel government gave the United States a 30-day deadline to jointly determine the new status of joint military bases. During this period, if the embargo was not lifted or negotiations did not begin, a unilateral decision would be made. On July 25, 1975, the Defense and Cooperation Agreement signed in 1969 was unilaterally terminated. With the termination, all joint military facilities and bases ceased their activities. All facilities came under the control and supervision of the Turkish Armed Forces. The U.S. was shocked by this unexpectedly tough decision. This very uncompromising decision had the signatures of Türkeş, who had been accused of being a NATO soldier for years, and Demirel, who was called "Morrison Süleyman." In a meeting with Ford at the Helsinki Leaders' Summit, Demirel rejected Ford's offer to halt the process in exchange for $50 million worth of military aid. After the meeting with Ford, Demirel's tone became increasingly harsh. On October 2, 1975, the Senate passed a law easing the embargo. This shifted from a complete embargo to a partial embargo. This development was followed by the signing of the U.S.-Turkey Defense Support Agreement on March 27, 1976. The said agreement would take effect once the embargo was lifted. The White House committed to providing Turkey with $1 billion in military support each year, with $200 million given as a grant. All facilities were to be under the command of Turkish officers, and most of the technical personnel would be selected from among the Turks. Thus, the AP-MHP-MSP government took full control of the bases under the complete administration of the United States, further solidifying its control in 1976. On one side, Türkeş and Demirel, who took a stance against the United States, took control of the bases under Turkish supervision, and deported American personnel, while on the other side, the leftist CHP putschists took the list provided by the United States, seized the retirement bonuses of the commanders and officers, and retired them, deeming them "American servants." Who do you think are the American stooges? The embargo was lifted 3.5 years later on September 26, 1978, when Ecevit was the Prime Minister. Ecevit did not follow a submissive policy like İnönü. He adopted a nationalist and honorable stance.

E-) THE TURKISH WORLD CONCEPT OF THE NATIONALIST MOVEMENT

In his work "Millî Doktrin Dokuz Işık," Türkeş expressed his views on the Turkish Union as follows: "... The ideal of the Turkish Union is the aspiration for all Turks on Earth to unite as one nation and state, under one flag. The realization of this may seem impossible at first glance to some individuals. Many may categorize it as a harmful fantasy. However, it is essential to remember that every truth begins with a dream. It is also crucial to recall that in 1919, the idea of embarking on a war in Anatolia against the victors of the world to establish an independent and free Turkey was also characterized as madness and a dream. Nevertheless, those who believed and dedicated themselves to an ideal succeeded in saving the homeland and establishing an independent Turkey. The idea of the Turkish Union will also become a reality one day through systematic work, seizing opportunities, and above all, striving to protect and elevate Turkey."

Since becoming the Chairman of the CKMP, Türkeş closely monitored developments in the Turkish world and maintained close contact with nationalist movements. He consistently made efforts to end the captivity of Turks in the Turkish world and secure their democratic rights and freedoms. Due to Türkeş's accumulated knowledge of the Turkish world, we see that he engaged in intense political activism after the dissolution of the Eastern Bloc. It was his duty to inform the Turkish public and guide governments in supporting Turkish communities. Prime Ministers and Presidents invited Türkeş to accompany them on their trips to Central Asia to benefit from his knowledge and connections. They conducted relations through him and facilitated some dialogues that he initiated. For example, Türkeş received great attention when he participated in Demirel's official visit to Central Asia. He was welcomed with affection in Azerbaijan and Turkmenistan.

Immediately after the dissolution of the Soviet Union, at the request of Türkeş and his associates, Türkeş's speeches in the general debate in the Turkish Grand National Assembly reflect the MHP's thoughts and suggestions regarding the Turkish world. Türkeş stated that Turkey closely concerned itself with the Turkish world, Iran, Arab countries, European countries, and the United States. The goal of the United States and European countries is to pressure Russia through Turkish communities and exploit Turkish territories. Iran and Arab countries have ideological objectives. Turkey has not been able to establish adequate economic, political, and cultural relations with Turkish communities. It is impossible to achieve results without a state policy; personal efforts alone are insufficient. Turkey will not be able to obtain the place it deserves in the emerging new world due to its insufficient policies. Türkeş emphasized that this issue had never been part of Turkish foreign policy before; foreign policy had been adjusted according to the Soviet Union. He expressed that there was fear in Turkey of bringing up Turkish communities politically outside of Turkey and that those who advocated dealing with Turkish communities were accused of pursuing a harmful agenda. Türkeş, who was an old friend with a long history in the political arena, stated that he had spent 55 years of his life dealing with these issues. According to recent statistics from the United Nations, Turkish ranks fifth among the most widely spoken languages on Earth. It comes fifth after Chinese, English, Spanish, and Arabic, which means that, according to this ranking, even though the Turkish nation has suffered many disasters, it is still one of the most populous nations on Earth. To say "200 million people speak Turkish" means to say "there are 200 million Turks." According to Türkeş, the most widely spoken fifth language in the world is Turkish. Some of those who speak Turkish are the Turks who remained in the regions from which the Ottoman Empire withdrew. Some of them are Turkic people in the USSR. With the dissolution of the Soviet Union, five Turkic republics gained independence. Besides these, there are Turkish communities in Russia. China may dissolve in the future, but the Ministry of Foreign Affairs shows no interest in these issues. However, considering the geopolitical position, economic value, and social structure of the Turkic republics, policies should be formulated. Rational and scientific policies should be established regarding Georgia and Armenia.

Türkeş's numerous speeches, in addition to the speech provided above, address the geopolitics of the Turkish world, with a particular focus on Georgia and Armenia. Türkeş was the first statesman to realize that these countries hindered the geographical integrity of Turkish states and to formulate strategies to solve this problem. In fact, Türkeş was aware of the necessity of geographical integrity for the rapid development of Turkish relations and continually emphasized this. The Zangezur Corridor, the Baku-Tbilisi-Ceyhan Oil Pipeline, and the Baku-Supsa Oil Pipeline projects were steps taken towards achieving geographical integrity. Türkeş did not live long enough to see his projects come to fruition. However, first Demirel and Aliyev, then Erdoğan and Aliyev, put the oil pipelines into operation and achieved much more. Georgia was economically integrated with Turkey and Azerbaijan, which also contributed to the formation of geographical integrity between Turkey and Azerbaijan. The economic relations of the three countries increased significantly. Due to Armenia's occupation of Azerbaijani territory, similar processes did not occur with Armenia. While Georgia prospered and enriched itself, Armenia, despite the money coming from the diaspora, became increasingly impoverished.

ome statesmen have characterized Azerbaijan Turks as Shia and leaning towards Iran, and these words have made both themselves and Azerbaijani Turks uncomfortable. Türkeş expressed that these people are our brothers in terms of ethnicity, religion, and culture. He noted that Azerbaijani Turks have warm feelings for Turkey and expect leadership from Turkey, emphasizing the need to reestablish Turkish foreign policy based on this axis. Türkeş mentioned that there were reports in newspapers suggesting that if we recognize Turkmenistan, we should also recognize Armenia, but the possible reactions in Azerbaijan, whose lands are under occupation, were not considered. Türkeş argued that Turkey's and fraternal Azerbaijan's interests should be considered. Türkeş stated that the newly independent republics wanted to use the same alphabet as Turkey but that the current alphabet with 29 letters did not meet their needs. He proposed adding five more letters to create a shared alphabet, highlighting the importance of a common alphabet for cultural unity, in line with Ismail Gaspıralı's motto of "Unity in Language, Thought, and Action."

According to Türkeş, to become a world power, Turkey needs to plan a policy of opening up to the world. Since its establishment, Turkey has focused on good relations with its neighbors, adhering to the principle of "Peace at home, peace in the world." Türkeş emphasized the need to reconsider foreign policy without deviating from this axis due to the changes and transformations in the Soviet Union. He noted that the dissolution of the USSR did not mean the elimination of the Slavic threat. Türkeş stressed the importance of being aware of the Russian population and influence in the Turkic republics and suggested dividing the Turkic republics into two categories: those located to the east and west of the Caspian Sea. Türkeş mentioned that those in the west of the Caspian Sea had close relations with Anatolia, and those in the east of the Caspian Sea were the Turkic people of Western Turkistan and the Idil-Ural Turks, with other Turkic communities in the east and northeast. He highlighted that recent developments had created new opportunities for Turkey and that preparations should be made to take advantage of these opportunities. While formulating policies, it is important not to create the perception that "a Turan Empire is desired" or that "Pan-Turkism is being pursued," and instead, policies should be developed without disturbing the global public.

Türkeş believed that Turkey needed to establish very close economic, political, and cultural relations with Azerbaijan, Kazakhstan, Kyrgyzstan, Turkmenistan, and Uzbekistan. He pointed out that the Turkic communities are identical to Turkey in terms of ethnicity, language, and religion (except for Gagauz, Chuvash, and Yakut Turks) and that close relations could be established. Türkeş also recommended paying close attention to other countries' interests in Turkic republics' underground and surface resources, especially Germany and the United States. According to Türkeş, we should not disregard the ideological approaches of Iran and Saudi Arabia, and it should not be assumed that Russia will easily give up these regions. Türkeş stated that Armenia, our neighbor, had a policy based on hostility towards Turks, and unless it abandoned this hostile attitude against Azerbaijan, friendship could not be established with Armenia. Türkeş drew attention to the ideological vacuum in Turkic republics and recommended that Turkey convey its peaceful, human rights-respecting, and brotherhood-based Islamic understanding to this region. He also mentioned the need to provide assistance to these regions, highlighting the colonial policies and troubles resulting from nuclear tests in Turkestan.

Türkeş pointed out the importance of preparing for these opportunities and emphasized the need to be cautious not to create the perception of a "Turan Empire" or "Pan-Turkism" but to develop policies without disturbing the international community.

On April 8, 1993, Türkeş, in an extraordinary speech in the Turkish Grand National Assembly (TBMM), emphasized the importance of protecting the borders of Azerbaijan, an independent state and a member of the United Nations. He stressed that at that time, 12% of Azerbaijani territories were under occupation, 300,000 Azerbaijani Turks were left homeless, and thousands of people had been killed. Türkeş pointed out that when Kuwait was occupied, the United Nations took action against Iraq, and the same sensitivity needed to be shown for Azerbaijan. He also highlighted that according to the principles of the Organization for Security and Cooperation in Europe, the existing borders and the territorial integrity of each state were guaranteed. Türkeş argued that this situation should not only apply to European states but also to Azerbaijan, and the occupation of Azerbaijan needed to be prevented. He stated that Turkey, as a state responsible for maintaining peace, should work to ensure peace in the region. Türkeş called for the Turkish Grand National Assembly to authorize the Turkish Armed Forces to take action beyond the borders. Additionally, he suggested that the legal dimension of the issue should be explained to the international community through diplomatic means, and Armenia's aggression must be ended.

On December 14, 1994, Türkeş proposed the establishment of a Ministry of Foreign Turks with a legislative proposal. In his proposal, he emphasized the need to take active interest in citizens living in countries like Western Europe, Saudi Arabia, Libya, and Kuwait. He noted that the Turks in Turkistan and the Caucasus, as well as those in Australia, were facing issues related to language, religious practices, social adaptation, and economic conditions. Türkeş stated that these issues needed to be actively addressed. Türkeş also mentioned that there were similar organizations in the UK, France, and elsewhere, such as the "Foreign and Commonwealth Office" and "DOM" in France, which served similar purposes. He recommended that Turks form similar cooperation organizations within the European Union, the Black Sea Economic Cooperation Organization, Nafta, and other international cooperation organizations.

Türkeş initiated the "Turkish States and Communities Friendship, Brotherhood, and Cooperation Congress," with its first meeting held in Ankara in March 1993. This congress aimed to bring the Turkic world together, promote joint projects and collaborations, and was endorsed as a celebration of the Nevruz Turkish holiday. Türkeş believed that significant changes were occurring in the world, where nations were coming together, regardless of race, culture, nationality, and ethnicity, opening the era of democracy, human rights, brotherhood, and cooperation in the 21st century. He emphasized that colonialism was inhumane and that the world had transitioned from an era of empire collapses and colonialism to an era of peace, and it was crucial for Turkic communities to establish collaboration similar to examples in other regions. Türkeş believed that such cooperation would lead to the development and prosperity of Turkic communities.

Türkeş emphasized that the close cooperation between Turkish communities was not intended to harm others but to promote peace, happiness, and prosperity through peaceful means. He noted that Turks in their respective regions had historically lived peacefully with their neighbors and stressed that Turkey's relations with Russia should be based on the principles of equal rights and non-interference in each other's internal affairs. Türkeş believed that many Turkic regions had been maintained as Russian colonies until the dissolution of the Soviet Union, but this situation needed to change. He called for Turks to establish a very strong and friendly collaboration with Russians based on principles that included the following:

1.   **Reciprocity Principle:** Every matter between the parties should be in the same measure, quality, and quantity.
2.   **Non-Interference in Internal Affairs:** The parties should respect each other's sovereignty and not interfere in each other's internal affairs.
3.   **Equality Principle:** In their relations, the parties should always be on equal terms.
4.   **Equal Rights:** The parties should always possess equal rights.

The Congress particularly highlighted the importance of a common language and alphabet. Türkeş stated in his closing speech that Turkic communities, which had not been able to come together for a thousand years, had finally come together. He emphasized that the saying of Ismail Gaspıralı, "Unity in Language, Thought, and Action," should always be the guiding light for Turks. Türkeş stressed the importance of Turkic communities that had gained independence to free themselves from ignorance and underdevelopment, develop economically and technologically, and integrate with the world. He believed that relationships with the West could be established with Turkey's assistance and that student and expert exchanges should take place among Turkic communities.

Türkeş suggested that Turkic communities should adopt the Latin alphabet quickly and transition to multi-party democratic regimes that respect human rights, the rule of law, and freedom. He believed that these steps were essential for their development and progress.

The 2nd Congress of Turkish States and Communities Friendship, Brotherhood, and Cooperation took place from October 20-23, 1994, in Izmir. Türkeş, in his address as the Honorary Chairman, noted that it was an era of advanced technology and globalization. He emphasized that Turkic states and communities needed to enhance their communication with the world to maintain their independence. Türkeş highlighted that the most developed countries belonged to the G7 group, and Turkey had close dialogue with these countries. He stressed that Turkic states and communities should also benefit from this experience. Türkeş pointed out several key areas to focus on:

1.   The importance of intellectual collaboration among Turkic states and communities, with joint projects led by universities.

2.   The establishment of information centers for the spread of modern technology and ensuring fast communication among Turkic states and communities.

3.   The existence of a significant computer deficit in Turkic states, which Turkey should help address.

4.   The necessity for Turkey to acquire nuclear technology.

5.   The need for Turkic states to run joint programs with Russia and Western countries as part of cooperation efforts.

6.   The significance of space research.

7.   The attraction of Western capital to Turkic states to bring their resources into their economies.

8.   Turkey's role in assisting Turkic states in joining international organizations.

9.   The establishment of a "Turkish Republics High Council" with the participation of Azerbaijan, Turkey, Kazakhstan, Uzbekistan, Turkmenistan, and Kyrgyzstan, rotating the presidency among their presidents every year, and forming a "Turkish Republics Cooperation Assembly" consisting of fifty members from each country.

10.   Adherence to the principle of reciprocity.

11.   Non-interference in internal affairs.

12.   Commitment to the principle of equality.

The final declaration of the 2nd Congress of Turkish States and Communities Friendship, Brotherhood, and Cooperation, held in Izmir from October 20-23, 1994, emphasized the importance of Turkic states independently pursuing their collaborations with each other. It highlighted that interference by third-party countries in these collaborations would constitute an interference in the internal affairs of these sovereign nations, which no independent country could accept.

During the III. Turkish States and Communities Friendship, Brotherhood, and Cooperation Congress, organized by the Turkish States and Communities Friendship, Brotherhood, and Cooperation Foundation and held in Izmir from September 30 to October 2, 1995, Türkeş, serving as the President-General of TÜDEV, delivered the opening speech. He stated that Turkish congresses had now institutionalized and become regular international meetings. The aim of the congress was to enhance the scientific, cultural, social, and political relationships between Turkish states, primarily with Russia, and other regional countries to improve the prosperity of these nations.

Türkeş emphasized that raising the living standards and increasing the welfare of Turkish communities relied on keeping up with the modern world in science and technology. Therefore, this issue was the main agenda of the congress. Efforts to develop student and scientist exchange programs between universities would be pursued to this end. Türkeş pointed out that elevating the standard of living was a guarantee of freedom for Turkish communities and that Turkey's relations with the European Union could be used for the benefit of Turkish states, thereby increasing their prosperity.

Türkeş also highlighted the importance of transporting the oil and natural gas of Azerbaijan and Western Turkistan countries to Europe via Turkey, suggesting the construction of the Baku-Ceyhan Pipeline as a critical step. He stressed that pipelines were crucial in contrast to the risks associated with fuel transportation via the Straits.

Türkeş underlined the need to swiftly implement the 34-letter common Turkic alphabet discussed at the 1st Congress and the importance of adopting the Latin alphabet to enhance integration among Turks and with the West, thus solidifying the independence of Turkish republics. Additionally, he once again emphasized the urgent creation of the "Turkish Republics High Council" with the participation of presidents from the Turkish republics and the "Turkish Republics Cooperation Assembly," consisting of fifty representatives from each country.

Türkeş also called for initiatives to make one of the Turkish states a permanent member of the UN Security Council. He emphasized the importance of Turkish states establishing close friendships and cooperation to elevate the region's prosperity and increase their trade volumes. Türkeş also addressed the issues of Western Thrace, Karabakh, Bosnia and Herzegovina, Chechnya, and the Turkmen in northern Iraq, advocating for the democratic rights and freedoms of the communities living there.

Drawing examples from organizations like NAFTA and the EU, Türkeş reiterated the need for the establishment of an economic union among Turkish states, emphasizing adherence to the principles of reciprocity, equality, and non-interference in internal affairs.

The focus of the IV. Congress of Turkish States and Communities Friendship, Brotherhood, and Cooperation, held on March 24, 1996, was on the importance of activities and measures to increase the influence and significance of Turkish republics in the international community. Türkeş emphasized the significance of six Turkish republics being UN members, suggesting that Turkish could also become an official language of the UN as its current official languages include English, French, Arabic, Spanish, and Russian. Thus, the immediate implementation of the 34-letter common Turkic alphabet from the 1st Congress was vital.

Türkeş also restated his proposal for the urgent creation of the "Turkish Republics High Council" and the "Turkish Republics Cooperation Assembly" with participation from the Turkish republics. He underscored the importance of Turkish states establishing close friendships and cooperation to elevate the region's prosperity and increase their trade volumes.

He invoked the example of the Commonwealth in terms of relations with Turkey's past imperial geography, suggesting that similar relations, based on equality and respect for sovereignty, could be established. Türkeş also mentioned the concept of the Great Turkestan Confederation, encompassing Kazakhstan, Kyrgyzstan, Turkmenistan, Uzbekistan, Tajikistan, Azerbaijan, the northern region of Afghanistan, and East Turkestan.

In a May 4, 1992 article in the Milliyet newspaper, Fikret Bila highlighted the significant influence of Türkeş in shaping Turkey's policies toward the Turkish world. Many structures and organizations related to the Turkish world and foreign Turks, such as the Turkish Council, drew from Türkeş's ideas and vision. The transformation of the Turkish Council into the Organization of Turkic States reflects the long-term vision of Türkeş, who proposed a common council with the participation of presidents or prime ministers of Turkish republics back in 1992.

Türkeş had a profound relationship with Ebulfez Elçibey, who played a key role in the independence struggle of Azerbaijan Turks. Both leaders were committed to the unity of the Turkish world and formulated policies accordingly. Elçibey held Türkeş in high regard and considered him his favorite leader. Türkeş delivered a speech in Baku's Azatlık Square on May 3, 1992, in support of Elçibey, which marked a significant moment in their relationship. In his speech, Türkeş emphasized the pursuit of freedom, independence, and human rights for the Turkish nation rather than seeking to establish empires or engage in colonialism. Elçibey consulted with Türkeş during his visits to Turkey, emphasizing the sincerity and shared objectives of their relationship. After Türkeş's passing, Elçibey expressed his respect in a telegram, acknowledging Türkeş's profound influence on the Turkish world.

Mustafa Cemil Kırımoğlu, the legendary leader of the Crimean Tatars, spoke highly of Türkeş's commitment to the Turkish world. He mentioned that he first heard of Türkeş in a Soviet train in 1973, realizing that Türkeş's party was held in high regard in Turkey despite the negative propaganda. Kırımoğlu expressed gratitude to Türkeş for his support and solidarity with the Crimean Tatars. Their embrace during the Turkish congresses held in Germany remains a vivid memory. Türkeş's remarks during those events underlined the mutual respect and love between the two leaders. Kırımoğlu also noted Türkeş's influence on the discussions surrounding the Organization of Turkic States.

These accounts demonstrate Türkeş's significant impact on the policies, relationships, and cooperation among Turkish states and communities. His forward-looking proposals and dedication to the Turkish world have had a lasting effect on the promotion of unity, cooperation, and shared values among Turkish-speaking nations.

The leader of the Turkish Cypriots, Rauf Denktaş, mentioned in the 1960s that they had meetings with the President, Prime Minister, and Foreign Minister of Turkey, and Alparslan Türkeş was also present at these meetings. During one of these meetings, Denktaş discussed the problems of Cyprus based on the plans of Makarios. Türkeş, after the meeting, assured Denktaş in a one-on-one conversation, saying, "Don't worry. Instead of sending weapons, we will send a Cypriot with a military background as an Ambassador. Makarios will not be given a chance." Türkeş's suggestion was implemented. The Demirel government issued a warning to Greece, leading to the withdrawal of the Greek army from the island. On the occasion of the first anniversary of Türkeş's passing, Rauf Denktaş sent a message to a symposium, which is as follows: "Recognizing

Alparslan Türkeş, a leader who has made his mark and left a trace in Turkish history and who collaborated with him on the Cyprus issue, will always be an honor for me. He was a great, courageous, resolute leader who took pride in the Turkish nation and worked tirelessly to protect Turkey's interests. May he rest in peace."

The method employed in handling the Cyprus issue was also applied in Western Thrace. Alparslan Türkeş, including Sadık Ahmet's meetings with senior Turkish officials in 1991.

Alparslan Türkeş is known as a great advocate for Isa Yusuf Alptekin. Türkeş often met with the late Alptekin, who is considered one of the symbolic figures of the independence and freedom struggle in East Turkestan. The statement "The starting point of our history, the main source of our culture, East Turkestan; is not only an issue for the thirty million people struggling for life in those lands but also a bitter but real issue for the entire world Turkic community. The East Turkestan issue came to the world's agenda 45 years ago with the precious person Isa Yusuf Alptekin, whom we buried in our soil last year, and has constituted the most important part of our External Turks issue from that day to this day."

Prof. Dr. Erşat Hürmüzlü, President of the Kirkuk Foundation, describes his introduction to the late Türkeş during his student years in Ankara as follows: "I was introduced to him by Acar Okan brother, and when we went to him, he told us to socialize as much as possible in all social places in Kirkuk; sports clubs, entertainment venues, where young people hang out, and also go to mosques. Because the more we socialize, the more we can influence society. In the end, he added this sentence: 'The greatest sacrifice is to endure defamation.' Because there are always jealousies, mischief, and divisions within society. He used this sentence to say that we shouldn't care about them. Nuri Gürgür stated, 'Regarding the unjust execution of Nejdet Koçak, the then Minister of Foreign Affairs met with the Iraqi Ambassador at the insistence of a political group that supported the government, referring to the late Türkeş.'"

Turkish nationalist movements, including the Nationalist Movement Party (MHP), are based on a nationalist understanding that emphasizes cultural, linguistic, and historical unity, rather than race. Turks, Kurds, Circassians, Albanians, Bosniaks, Laz people, regardless of their ethnic origin, are considered essential components of the nation, primarily in Anatolia and Thrace. These groups have integrated over time to constitute the Turkish nation. MHP was concerned with the issues of Turks living as citizens in states such as Russia, China, Iran, Iraq, and Afghanistan and expressed this concern, raising slogans like "The Enslaved Turkish Lands," "Freedom to Turkestan," and "All Turks are One Army." These approaches were risky, both for Turkey and the mentioned Turkish peoples, but they were deemed necessary to maintain the spirit of the Turkish nation. Right-wing governments underlined the importance of good neighborly relations and showed it through their actions. They supported the Kazakhs who escaped Soviet oppression, and the Uyghurs who suffered under Chinese rule, providing them with refuge in specific regions and granting them citizenship. The same approach was applied to the immigrants from Rumelia. Many of the significant political figures, who played a role in this policy's implementation, had immigrant backgrounds, which influenced their stance. Bayar and Demirel were of Rumelian descent, and Menderes's family had Crimean roots. Erdogan's family came from the Caucasus.

The policy implemented by right-wing governments also had a significant impact when the USSR, the Eastern Bloc, and Yugoslavia dissolved. The Turkic Republics, the peoples of the Caucasus and the Balkans who gained independence saw Turkey as a brotherly country and accepted it because they had relatives, acquaintances, neighbors, and friends in Turkey. This perspective gave Ankara more room to maneuver and brought an end to three centuries of isolation, strengthening Turkey. Would this have happened if right-wing governments hadn't embraced Turkish communities abroad and followed a policy of good neighborly relations? CHP, for example, failed to support Turkic immigrants in the Boratan Bridge incident, where 195 Azerbaijani Turks who sought refuge in our country were handed over to the Soviets and were killed on the bridge before they could cross. In Saudi Arabia, nearly half a million Turkistanis live, mostly Uzbeks. They fled the oppressive policies of the communist regime. Because CHP did not support Turkistanis, they had to settle there.

Ülkücüler, an understanding of nationalism based on culture, language, and historical unity, rather than race. Turks, Kurds, Circassians,

Albanians, Bosniaks, Laz people, regardless of whether they have Turkish roots, are considered essential components of the nation. These elements, primarily in Anatolia and Rumelia, have merged and formed a nation. The Nationalist Movement Party (MHP) addressed the problems of Turks living as citizens in states such as Russia, China, Iran, Iraq, and Afghanistan, and brought them to the forefront. Slogans like "Captive Turkish Lands," "Freedom to Turkestan," and "All Turks are One Army" were voiced. Such approaches were risky for both Turkey and the mentioned Turkish peoples but were deemed necessary to preserve the spirit of the Turkish nation. The international community needed to know that external Turks were not left helpless. MHP placed importance on good neighborly relations. Right-wing governments showed their stance through their actions. They supported Kazakhs escaping Soviet oppression and Uyghurs suffering under Chinese rule, providing them refuge in specific regions and granting them citizenship. The same approach was applied to immigrants from Rumelia. All immigrants from Rumelia were embraced and granted citizenship, a result of the adopted nationalist perspective. Turkish communities in Western Thrace and Bulgaria, Bosniaks, and Albanians in Yugoslavia, as well as Turks and Tatars in Romania, saw Turkey as both a sanctuary and homeland. When the USSR, the Eastern Bloc, and Yugoslavia dissolved, these newly independent Turkic republics and the peoples of the Caucasus and the Balkans accepted Turkey as a brotherly country, as they had relatives, acquaintances, neighbors, and friends in Turkey. This perspective provided Ankara with more room for maneuver and ended three centuries of isolation, strengthening Turkey. If right-wing governments had not embraced Turkish communities abroad and pursued a policy of good neighborly relations, would this have been possible? CHP, for example, handed over 195 Azerbaijani Turks who sought refuge in Turkey to the Soviets in the Boratan Bridge incident, and they were killed on the bridge. Nearly half a million Turkestanis live in Saudi Arabia, mostly Uzbeks. Turkestanis had to settle there because CHP did not support them.

When the Soviet Union disappeared in 1991, nearly thirty countries gained their independence. The breakup of the USSR, along with the disintegration of Yugoslavia, occurred while Turgut Özal was President and Süleyman Demirel was Prime Minister, with both leaders engaging in a competitive rivalry. However, they acted in concert regarding the Turkic world because Alparslan Türkeş had already laid out the path to follow.

The MHP and its affiliated organizations were best equipped to handle external Turkish affairs, as they had the knowledge, experience, and policies for it. The MHP took ownership of the Turkic republics, providing loans and grants where possible, and delivering requested essential supplies. Tens of thousands of students were brought to Turkey for education. Universities were established in Kazakhstan (Ahmet Yesevi) and Kyrgyzstan (Manas). Great efforts were made to improve trade relations. The strategy of Turkey becoming an energy hub was initiated by right-wing administrations. Türkeş and Abulfaz Elchibey were the first to bring the Baku-Ceyhan Oil Pipeline project to the table. When Türkeş suggested that the pipeline pass through Armenia, Elchibey was shocked. Türkeş argued that if the pipeline went through there, Armenia would be unable to maintain its previous extremism. Demirel, a leader who played a key role in the project, established personal friendships with leaders from the Turkic world, which proved instrumental in solving issues. For instance, when Demirel learned that Reşat Javadov, the commander of the Azerbaijani Special Military Unit OMON, was planning a coup against Heydar Aliyev, he informed Aliyev, who thwarted the coup. After this incident, relations with Azerbaijan improved significantly. Under Aliyev and Erdoğan, the two countries drew even closer. The Trans-Anatolian Pipeline (TANAP) project was realized. Azerbaijan made investments such as the Star Oil Refinery in Izmir. With the Star investment, Azerbaijan completed its third major project after the Baku-Tbilisi-Ceyhan pipeline and TANAP. The Trans-Adriatic Pipeline (TAP), completed in 2021, made Azerbaijan a major gas supplier to Eastern Europe. Full support was provided to Azerbaijan during the Second Nagorno-Karabakh War, and Azerbaijan reclaimed a significant portion of its occupied territories. The ceasefire agreement between Azerbaijan and Armenia included a clause specifying the opening of the Zangezur Corridor between Nakhchivan and Azerbaijan, a highly strategic development in terms of the geographical integrity of the Turkic world. Türkeş had first introduced the Zangezur Corridor to the agenda in the early 1990s, but Armenia's occupation of 20% of Azerbaijani territory had pushed it aside. During the Second Nagorno-Karabakh War, Bahçeli reintroduced this critical issue to the agenda. It was emphasized that the Zangezur Corridor should be included in both the ceasefire and peace agreements. As a result of the efforts made, Turkey and Azerbaijan became each other's major trading partners. After three decades, the goal of being "one nation, two states" was fully realized. Under the guidance of Aliyev and Demirel, Georgia was integrated into the economies of both countries using delicate diplomacy. Thanks to the developed bilateral relations, Turkish construction companies became the most active businesses in Central Asia and Azerbaijan. Demirel, through his initiatives, convinced Ukraine to recognize the establishment of the Crimean Tatar National Assembly in Crimea, which resulted in increased returns to Crimea, which is considered the homeland of the Tatars. Additionally, Demirel was instrumental in Moldova recognizing Gagauzia as an Autonomous Republic. This prevented bloodshed and provided constitutional guarantees to Gagauzia. Without Demirel's guidance, Gagauzia might have become a place disconnected from the international community, much like Transnistria, Crimea, Donbas, Abkhazia, and South Ossetia.

Demirel's statement, "The Turkish World is born from the Adriatic to the Great Wall of China," strongly emphasizes the right-wing's concept of "Turk." When the Adriatic is considered the border, it underscores that Albanians and Bosniaks are also parts of the Turkish nation. Turgut Özal, on the other hand, laid out Turkey's vision for the near future by saying, "The 21st century will be the Turkish century." In line with this description and vision, Ankara gave the harshest response to the massacre of Bosniaks by Serbs and Croats in Bosnia and Herzegovina. Demirel stirred international public opinion and rallied support. Alparslan Türkeş visited Bosnia and Herzegovina multiple times. He met with Alija Izetbegović, offering open support. The MHP organized rallies across the country to make the Bosnian issue a national concern, similar to Cyprus. Tansu Çiller, in the face of the attacks and bombings of Sarajevo from both land and air, challenged the enemy and drew international attention to the issue by visiting Sarajevo. Following her trip to Bosnia, NATO actively intervened in the massacre. Erdoğan displayed a similar approach to the killings by Serbs in Kosovo. Erdoğan played a significant role in Kosovo gaining its independence. Thanks to the strategies implemented by Türkeş and Bahçeli and the resulting circumstances, the "Turkish World," which was only on the agenda of the Nationalist Movement in the 1970s and 1980s, eventually became a topic of interest for the entire Turkish population.

Erdoğan and Bahçeli further developed the Turkish World policies shaped by Türkeş, Özal, and Demirel. Erdoğan's pursuit of an independent foreign policy, his willingness to confront the United States, and his establishment of good relations with Russia expanded Turkey's maneuvering space in Central Asia and the Caucasus. In the years immediately following 1991, Russia considered Turkey's activities in the region as American activities and acted accordingly. Under Erdoğan's rule, Turkey became further estranged from the United States. TURKPA and the Turkish Academy were established during Erdoğan's tenure. The "Turkish-Speaking Countries' Presidential Summits," which used to be held on an annual basis with the participation of the presidents of four Turkish states, evolved into the Turkish Council. Uzbekistan and Hungary joined the Council. In 2021, the Turkish Council was renamed the Turkish States Organization (TSO). By softening its thirty-year policy in Turkmenistan, the organization was allowed to join as an observer member. The TSO is a comprehensive and active organization that includes sub-units and executive authorities. Ankara, which was unable to achieve its goals in the Shanghai Cooperation Organization (SCO) and the G-8, successfully implemented a strategic project despite all obstacles with the establishment and structuring of the TSO. The strategic moves of Autonomous Turkish Republics such as Tatarstan, Bashkortostan, Khakassia, Sakha, Tuva, Altai, and Gagauzia joining TURKSOY are highly significant. This initiated a process of rapprochement with vast geographies beyond the Turkish Republics. When evaluating the 22-year rule of the AK Party, it will be seen that giving priority to the Turkish world was a recent development due to the collaboration with the MHP. The MHP not only supports the development of relations but also actively participates in determining and implementing the strategies, being equally vocal and influential as the AK Party.

F-) THE COMMON DESTINY OF TÜRKEŞ AND BAHÇELİ

In the 1991 elections, the Nationalist Movement Party (MÇP) formed an alliance with the Welfare Party (RP) and the Democratic Party (İDP) to overcome the 10% national threshold and regional thresholds. Running on RP lists, the MÇP won 19 parliamentary seats, making a comeback to the parliament after an eleven-year hiatus. No single party was able to secure a majority in the elections. Süleyman Demirel, the leader of the True Path Party (DYP), which received the most votes, formed a coalition government with the Social Democratic Populist Party (SHP). However, the MÇP's parliamentary group and Central Executive Board (MKYK) had differences of opinion on how to vote for the government. The norm was for opposition parties to cast negative votes. But, based on Türkeş's suggestion, the MHP leadership decided to vote in favor. The faction led by Muhsin Yazıcıoğlu opposed this decision. It was normal for those who did not agree with the proposal to oppose it, but after the decision was made, party discipline required them to act in line with the decision. However, Yazıcıoğlu and his followers did not do so. They abstained from the vote. This disagreement led to Yazıcıoğlu and his team leaving the party and forming the Great Unity Party. Their reasons and attitudes were quite clear. The MÇP was in opposition, while the SHP, which included far-left and separatist elements, was in government. The Nationalist Movement had fought against far-left elements before 1980 because they were seen as neither native nor national. They had external support and were divided into various far-left factions, controlled by communist states like the Soviet Union, China, Albania, and Yugoslavia. Particularly the USSR aimed for a regime change in Turkey. Before the March 12 Memorandum, the streets were heated, and a coup led by left-leaning officers was planned. This coup was scheduled for March 9. After the coup, Doğan Avcıoğlu was going to become the Prime Minister, and Turkey would withdraw from NATO. Subsequently, the country would first invite Soviet experts and then the Red Army. When MİT exposed the coup plan, the two military commanders who were going to lead the March 9 coup were stopped. Subsequently, the army issued the March 12 Memorandum. After the memorandum, the Soviet sympathizers within the army were purged. Those belonging to the civilian wing of the left-wing coup were arrested, tried, and sentenced. Communist youth leaders were either killed, executed, or imprisoned. Those who could escape went abroad. When looking back from today to the past, the project implemented by the Soviets before 1980 may not seem plausible. However, the Soviets successfully used similar methods in countries like Afghanistan, Egypt, Iraq, Yemen, and many others.

In the 1991 context, the USSR had collapsed, and the Eastern Bloc had disintegrated. Communism was no longer a threat to the country. Therefore, there was no longer any meaning in the struggle of the nationalists against far-left ideologies. Moreover, the SHP, in the center-left, was the successor of the Republican People's Party (CHP). The MHP had tried to establish good relations with center-left parties during the periods when it fought against the far-left as well. It had supported what it considered beneficial for the country by the CHP. For instance, it had supported the Cyprus intervention and the liberalization of poppy cultivation. The MHP ensured that the CHP's Cahit Karakaş became the Speaker of the Parliament in the parliamentary presidency elections, thereby lowering the tension in the country. Before 1980, the major threat to Turkey was communism, and the Nationalists fought against the communists. After 1980, the major threat was separatist terrorism. The Nationalist Movement was the primary ally of the state in the fight against separatist terrorism. In other words, Türkeş thought as follows: The Soviets had disintegrated, and many Turkish republics had gained their independence. Helping these republics, establishing good relations with them, and developing collaborations should be a priority. For Turkey, the major threat was the PKK. A comprehensive fight against the PKK should be waged. The MHP, which already had enough votes, decided to support the DYP-SHP government that was going to be established, even if they cast negative votes. SHP had separatist elements within it. MHP's support helped SHP, and thus the government, break free from the influence of these elements. Those within the SHP who supported the separatist terrorist organization were first expelled from the party, then arrested and tried. The ones who managed to survive fled abroad. Since the end of the 1980s, the Soviet project of before 1980 might not seem plausible when looking back from today. However, at that time, the Soviets aimed to destabilize Turkey first and then change its regime by inciting anarchy, terrorism, strikes, protests, and school occupations. The primary target of communist terrorism was the nationalists. Therefore, from 1970 to 1980, the nationalists had to defend both their country and themselves. The result was the September 12 coup. The communists did not achieve their goal. The coup makers, without distinguishing between the nationalists and communists, that is, by equating those who broke the jug with those who carried the jug, suppressed the parties involved in the most severe manner. The coup makers were planning to allow only a center-right and a center-left party in the new period. Perhaps a liberal party could have been allowed as well. But there was no room for nationalists in the new period. They had to be suppressed to the extent that they would never have an interest in politics again. They should not establish a nationalist party. When looking from the present to the past, the project implemented by the Soviets before 1980 may not seem plausible. However, the Soviets successfully used similar methods in countries like Afghanistan, Egypt, Iraq, Yemen, and many others.

In the 1991 context, the USSR had collapsed, and the Eastern Bloc had disintegrated. Communism was no longer a threat to the country. Therefore, there was no longer any meaning in the struggle of the nationalists against far-left ideologies. Moreover, the SHP, in the center-left, was the successor of the Republican People's Party (CHP). The MHP had tried to establish good relations with center-left parties during the periods when it fought against the far-left as well. It had supported what it considered beneficial for the country by the CHP. For instance, it had supported the Cyprus intervention and the liberalization of poppy cultivation. The MHP ensured that the CHP's Cahit Karakaş became the Speaker of the Parliament in the parliamentary presidency elections, thereby lowering the tension in the country. Before 1980, the major threat to Turkey was communism, and the Nationalists fought against the communists. After 1980, the major threat was separatist terrorism. The Nationalist Movement was the primary ally of the state in the fight against separatist terrorism. In other words, Türkeş thought as follows: The Soviets had disintegrated, and many Turkish republics had gained their independence. Helping these republics, establishing good relations with them, and developing collaborations should be a priority. For Turkey, the major threat was the PKK.

Türkeş faced a second attempt in 1992 to divide the Nationalist Movement Party (MÇP). Following legal changes allowing the reopening of closed parties, MÇP aimed to merge with the National Salvation Party (MSP), and they wanted to change the name of MÇP. On the other hand, a significant portion of MÇP members, mostly affiliated with the Motherland Party (ANAP), wanted to re-establish the MHP (Nationalist Movement Party) under the leadership of Şadi Somuncuoğlu.

The main goal of both attempts was to challenge Türkeş himself, as he represented the essence of Turkish nationalism in the political sphere. However, these attempts were mainly driven by the desire of Turgut Özal, who was a strong supporter of both initiatives. Özal sought to diminish Türkeş's influence within the Turkish nationalist movement, and if possible, eliminate it altogether. He was in favor of a "democratic solution" to address the Kurdish issue, and even open to the idea of a federation as a solution.

Türkeş's support for the DYP-SHP government led to a division within the MÇP ranks, just as Bahçeli's support for the AKP (Justice and Development Party) would do later on. Türkeş was supportive of the government's firm stance against the PKK (Kurdistan Workers' Party) during this period, while Bahçeli's MHP played a crucial role in supporting the government's counterterrorism efforts in the aftermath of the breakdown of the peace process. This strong backing of the government by the MHP eventually led to the establishment of an anti-terrorist strategy that has helped to mitigate the PKK's influence and control in Turkey.

In the end, these political divisions and actions have had far-reaching consequences for the Turkish political landscape and the country's approach to its domestic and foreign policy challenges.

G-) TÜRKEŞ AND BAHÇELİ'S THOUGHTS ON KURDS

Alpaslan Türkeş's inclusive nationalist approach is expressed through some of the following quotes:

- "A Turk and a Kurd are like flesh and nail; we have intermarried, and the more Turkish we are, the more they are Kurdish, and the more Kurdish they are, the more Turkish we are. Kurds are our own siblings; we love and care for them more than anyone else. They are Muslims, and we all prostrate to the same direction. We are all the ummah of the same prophet and are bound by the same holy book."

- "Laz, Kurd, Circassian, Abkhazian, Chechen are the branches of a single tree. The name of this tree is Turk. If you separate Kurds, Laz, Arabs, and Circassians from us, what will remain? A dry and leafless tree! In short, we would prepare our own downfall."

In the days leading up to his passing, Türkeş reminded the public of what Ziya Gökalp wrote in the June 1922 issue of "Küçük Mecmua" (Little Magazine): "If there is a Turk who doesn't love Kurds, he is not a Turk; if there is a Kurd who doesn't love Turks, he is not a Kurd."

Türkeş strongly criticized the unfortunate writings of Nihal Atsız, which denigrated Kurds. It was actually due to their differing views on this issue that Türkeş and his longtime comrade went their separate ways. Türkeş emphasized keeping discipline among the Idealists (Ülkücüler) and mentioned that DEP members should have control over their bases. During a meeting with the DEP delegation in 1992, Türkeş stated: "We have been brothers for 900 years. My nephews are Kurds. My sister is married to a Kurd. It is impossible for us to separate from each other..."

Türkeş's words showed the unifying and inclusive nature of the Idealist (Ülkücü) ideology, which aimed to bring people together. He stated that it was their priority to maintain discipline and unity among the Idealists and that DEP members should also be influential within their own communities. Türkeş's message was to prevent any internal conflict and to ensure that Turkey would not become an arena for external intervention.

It is clear from these expressions that Idealism (Ülkücülük) is unifying and inclusive, rather than divisive. Türkeş's inclusive nationalism is continued by Devlet Bahçeli, who emphasizes that Turkish nationalism is not based on religion, language, race, or sect, and rejects all forms of discrimination and exclusion.

References:

Melih Çoban, "Milliyetçilik Teorileri", *Türk Yurdu*, Mart 2012, sayı.295

Yosef Lapid, "Culture's Ship: Returns and Departures in International Relations Theory", *Return of Culture and Identity in IR Theory* (Eds. Yosef Lapid,Friedrich Kratochwil) içinde, UK: Lynne Rienner Publishers, 1996, s.4

Benedict Anderson, *Imagined Communities*. London: Verso, 1991, ss.64-65

Oral Sander, *Siyasi Tarih I*. Ankara: İmge Kitabevi, 1997, ss.114-115, 161-162

Ernest Gellner, *Nations and Nationalism: New Perspectives on the Past*. Oxford: Basic Blackwell Publisher, 1983, ss.98-99

Ku Klux Klan örgütünün yirminci yüzyıl başlarında 4 ila 5 milyon arasında üyesi olduğu tahmin ediliyordu. Ayrıntılı bilgi için bkz. http://en.wikipedia.org/wiki/Ku_Klux_Klan

William L. Shirer, Nazi İmparatorluğu I. İstanbul: İnkılap Kitabevi, 2002, s.305

Eric Hobsbawm, *1780'den Günümüze Milletler ve Milliyetçilik: Program, Mit, Gerçeklik.* İstanbul: Ayrıntı Yayınları, 1995, ss.173-179

Andrew Heywood, Politics. New York: Palgrave, 2002, ss.116-117

Deniz Vardar, Aşırı Sağdan Popülist Radikal Sağa: Fransa Örneği. İstanbul: Bağlam Yayınları, 2004, s.135

21. Yüzyılda Milliyetçilik. İletişim Yayınları: İstanbul. ANDERSON, B.(1995).

Hayali Cemaatler: Milliyetçiliğin Kökenleri ve Yayılması.(Çev. İ. Savaşır). Metis Yayınları: İstanbul.

AKADEMİK YAKLAŞIMLAR DERGİSİ JOURNAL OF ACADEMIC APPROACHES KIŞ 2018 CİLT: 9 SAYI:2 WINTER 2018 VOLUME: 9 ISSUE: 2 107 AKTÜRK, Ş.(2006).

Etnik Kategori ve Milliyetçilik: Tek etnili, Çok Etnili ve Gayri Etnik Rejimler. Doğu – Batı Dergisi. Ankara. Yıl:9, Sayı: 38. ALTUN,F.(2005).

Modernleşme Kuramı: Eleştirel Bir Giriş. Ankara: Küre Yayınları. BERKTAY, H.(2010).

Özgürlük Dersleri. Kitap yayınevi: İstanbul. CARR, E., H. (2015). Milliyetçilik ve Sonrası. (Çev. O. Akınhay). İletişim Yayıncılık: İstanbul.

ÇALIK, M.(2016). Milli Kimlik, Milliyet, Milletçilik. Cedit Neşriyat: Ankara. ÇITAK, Z.(2006).

Fransa'da Laiklik ve Milliyetçilik. Ankara: Doğu Batı Yayınları.

FUKUYAMA, F.(2012). Tarihin Sonu ve Son İnsan. (Çev. Z. Dicleli). Profil Yayınları: İstanbul.

GELLNER, E. (2008). Uluslar ve Ulusçuluk.(Çev. G.G. Özdoğan). Hil Yayınları: İstanbul.

GIDDENS, A.(2013). Sosyoloji. Kırmızı Yayınları: Ankara. HALDUN, İ. (2016).

Devlet. (Çev. O. Arpaçukuru). İlke Yayıncılık: İstanbul.

HEYWOOD, A.(2013). Siyaset. Adres Yayınları: Ankara. HOBSBAWM, E.(1995).

1780'den Günümüze Milletler ve Milliyetçilik-Program, Mit, Gerçeklik. (Çev. O. Akınhay). Ayrıntı Yayınları: İstanbul.

KARPAT, H. , K. (2012). Türk Dış Politikası. Timaş Yayınları: İstanbul. MANN, M. (2012).

Demokrasinin Karanlık Yüzü: Etnik Temizliği Açıklamak. (Çev. B. O. Doğan).

İthaki Yayınları: İstanbul. ORAN, B. (1997).

Az Gelişmiş Ülke Milliyetçiliği: Kara Afrika Modeli. Bilgi Yayınevi: Ankara. ORAN, B. (2001).

Küreselleşme ve Azınlıklar. İmaj Yayıncılık: Ankara. ÖZKAZANÇ, A.(2016).

Siyaset.(Edt. Y. Taşkın). İletişim Yayınları: İstanbul. ÖZKIRIMLI, U.(2015).

Milliyetçilik Kuramları: Eleştirel Bir Bakış. Doğu- Batı Yayınları: Ankara. RENAN, E.(1946).

Discours et Conferences. (Ç. Z. Ishan). Sakarya Basımevi: Ankara. RITZER, G.(2011).

Küresel Dünya.(Çev. M. Pekdemir). Ayrıntı Yayınları: İstanbul. SANDER, O. (2007).

Siyasi Tarih: 1918-1994. İmge Kitabevi: Ankara. SMITH, A. (1994).

Milli Kimlik.(Çev. B. Şener). İletişim Yayınları: İstanbul. SMITH, A. (2002).

Ulusların Etnik Kökeni. (Çev. S. Bayramoğlu, H. Kendir). Dost kitabevi: Ankara. SMITH, A.(2017).

Etno- Sembolizm ve Milliyetçilik. (Çev. B.F. Çallı). Alfa Araştırma: İstanbul.

AKADEMİK YAKLAŞIMLAR DERGİSİ JOURNAL OF ACADEMIC APPROACHES KIŞ 2018 CİLT: 9 SAYI:2   WINTER 2018 VOLUME: 9 ISSUE: 2 108 TOK, N. (2003).

Kültür, Kimlik ve Siyaset. Ayrıntı Yayınları: İstanbul. WALLERSTEIN, I. (1996).

Tarihsel Kapitalizm. (Çev. N. Alpay). Metis Yayıncılık: İstanbul. WALLERSTEIN, I. (2014).

Dünya Sistemleri Analizi.(Çev. E. Abadoğlu, N. Ersoy). Bgst Yayınları: İstanbul. WALLERSTEIN, I. (2015).

Jeopolitik ve Jeokültür. (Çev. M. Özel). Küre Yayınları: İstanbul. YALÇINER, R.(2014).

Etnisite ve Milliyetçilik: Eleştirel Bir Değerlendirme. Ankara Üniversitesi Sosyal Bilimler Fakültesi Dergisi.69, (1). 189-215. YANIK, C. (2013).

Etnisite, Kimlik ve Milliyetçilik Kavramlarının Sosyolojik Analizi. Kaygı 2013/ 20. YILDIRIM, E. (2014).

Modernite ve Milliyetçilik: Modern Milliyetçilik Kuramları Üzerine. Akademik Sosyal Araştırmalar Dergisi. Yıl:2. Sayı: 6. s.23.27

Kemal Can, "Ülkücü Hareketin İdeolojisi", Modern Türkiye'de Siyasi Düşünce, Cilt 4,

Milliyetçilik içinde, (Der.: Tanıl Bora ve Murat Gültekingil, İletişim Yayınları, 2009.

Hüdavendigar Onur, S. Ahmet Arvasi Kronolojisi, Biyografi Net Yayınları, 2011.

Helmut Dubiel, Yeni-Muhafazakârlık Nedir, (Çev.: Erol Özbek), İletişim Yayınları, 1998.

Tanıl Bora, Türk Sağının Üç Hali, Birikim Yayınları, 2010.

Osman Turan, Türkiye'de Siyasi Buhranın Kaynakları, İstanbul, Turan Neşriyat Yurdu, 1969, s. 8.

memleket SiyasetYönetim (MSY), Cilt 9, Sayı 22, Temmuz 2014, s. 377-399. 384

Nurettin Topçu, Ahlak Nizamı, Dergâh Yayınları, 1999, s. 303.

Yüksel Taşkın, Anti-Komünizmden Küreselleşme Karşıtlığına Milliyetçi-Muhafazakâr Entelijansiya, İletişim, 2007, s. 146-147. 1980 Öncesi Ülkücü Hareketin İslamileşmesinde Seyit Ahmet Arvasi Etkisi ve "Türk-İslam Ülküsü"

İbrahim Kafesoğlu, Türk-İslam Sentezi, Ötüken Yayınları, 1999, s. 149. s. 105. s. 110. s. 102.

S. Ahmet Arvasi, Türkiye'de Şark Meselesi ve Alınacak Tedbirler, Bilge Oğuz Yayınları, 2009.